New Directions *for* Youth Ministry

Loveland, Colorado

New Directions for Youth Ministry

Copyright © 1998 Group Publishing, Inc.

CREDITS

Contributing Authors: Cathi Basler; Harvey F. Carey; Chap Clark, Ph.D.; John R. Cutshall; Pamela J. Erwin; Monty L. Hipp; Mikal Keefer; Wayne Rice; John Ruhlman; and Mark H. Senter III
Editor: Amy Simpson
Creative Development Editor: Dave Thornton
Chief Creative Officer: Joani Schultz
Copy Editor: Janis Sampson
Designer and Art Director: Jean Bruns
Computer Graphic Artist: Nighthawk Design and Eris Klein
Cover Art Director: Jeff A. Storm
Cover Designer: Lisa Chandler
Photographer: Craig DeMartino
Illustrator: Eris Klein
Production Manager: Gingar Kunkel

Library of Congress Cataloging-in-Publication Data

New Directions for youth ministry
      p.   cm.
   ISBN 0-7644-2103-4
    1. Church group work with youth.   I. Group Publishing.
BV4447.N435   1998
259' .23--dc21

98-7059
CIP

10 9 8 7 6 5 4   07 06 05 04 03 02 01

Printed in the United States of America.
Visit our Web site: www.grouppublishing.com

Contents

Introduction

MARK H. SENTER III

Vice President of the Division of Open Studies and Associate Professor of Christian Education at Trinity International University in Deerfield, Illinois

I think it was the late Speaker of the House Tip O'Neill who said all politics are local. It's true: National elections are won or lost around local issues and the ability of local political leaders to gain the votes needed to support their candidates. National candidates are elected when local volunteers find ways to get enough votes on election day.

In a similar fashion, *all youth ministry is local.* No matter what the youth ministry specialists from the denominational headquarters say, the seminar leaders at youth ministry conferences promote, or the trainers from Christian ministries explain, youth ministry is only effective when it is a response to local needs guided by local convictions in the hands of local people. Community concerns and convictions, financial and leadership resources, theological and moral values, when tied to ministry vision and passion, shape strategies for reaching young people.

In the following pages, we will explore some new directions in youth ministry by focusing on some fascinating local models and strategies. Over the past twenty years, I have described the dominant youth ministry models in a general manner.[1] My intent was to explain the *families* of youth ministry options. This book is different. Here we will look at actual models as explained by people who are using them.

Misunderstandings About Models

Before looking at the models we have chosen for this book, let me put two misunderstandings of youth ministry to rest. First, ***relational youth ministry is not a distinct model.*** Any type of youth ministry that has been effective in the past two centuries has been relational in the context of the day. From the Sunday school classes of D.L. Moody to the Society for Christian Endeavor meetings of Francis Clark, from the Young Life Clubs of Jim Rayburn to the Student Impact of Bo Boshers, a primary key to effectiveness has been that young people have felt loved and accepted by peers and by the adults who led them.

Jesus Christ modeled incarnational ministry. In the first chapter of John, the apostle captures the essence of relational ministry: "The Word became flesh and made his dwelling among us" (1:14). At the very core of Christ's ministry was his presence with people. He spent time with them. He walked on their turf. He spoke their language. He ate their food. He felt their feelings. This was not a model of ministry; it was how God did ministry in human form. Other than some rare prophetic ministries (which Christ also exemplified), relational ministry is a nonnegotiable principle of all ministry.

It is easy to accuse highly programmed ministries of not being relational. Yet Student Impact at Willow Creek Community Church, the most highly programmed ministry in North America today, is both purpose driven and *fanatically relational.* Program is not the enemy of relationship in youth ministry. In fact, the only way a program will grow beyond thirty to forty in attendance is for leaders to structure (program) relational strategies into everything they do.

One of the great dangers in a postmodern age, when young people are clamoring for no-strings-attached relationships, is for youth ministers to check their Christianity at the door in an attempt to be relational. In their desire to be authentic, some Christian adults merely want to hang out with adolescents in the hope that their faith will cause their young friends to ask faith questions, even though matters of faith have not otherwise been discussed. Frankly, there is no biblical precedent for this strategy of ministry. Even in the pre-Christian era, when relationships were defined by rigid Greco-Roman customs or hypocritical Hebrew legalisms, Christ and the apostles always were the intentional initiators of conversations related to faith issues.

A second correction is ***small groups are nothing new.*** Every type of youth ministry that has been effective in transforming lives for Jesus Christ has had small groups somewhere in the mix. Sometimes they took the form of prayer meetings or Bible studies; at other times (believe it or not) they were committee meetings, planning teams, or officers meetings. Methodists called them class meetings, but they functioned much like accountability groups. Youth for Christ, in their

Campus Life strategy, implemented small groups that served many of the functions of meta groups (in the meta model, small groups are the primary mode of ministry and give birth to new groups as they grow). Even the work teams of student leaders at Young Life camps were forms of discipleship groups.

It is interesting that one of the greatest enemies of effective youth ministry over the years has been cliques, which are nothing more than small groups turned sour. Small groups are described as cliques when peers feel excluded. The spiritual bond that motivates clusters of young people to spend time together degenerates rather quickly into social bonds that have little if any outward focus. The cliquish small group becomes an end in itself.

Yet it is nearly impossible to build and sustain any model of youth ministry without a purposeful, well-shepherded system of spiritual accountability within a network of small groups. Spiritual accountability is both individual and collective. Individual students have a place where they know and are known, a safe place which allows vulnerability and requires action. The safety gives them freedom to talk about their fears and doubts, their hopes and dreams, their successes and failures without danger of rejection.

By keeping the group purpose driven, the collective group avoids falling prey to the social needs of individual students. The cluster of adolescents has a vision bigger than itself, a goal that all members share, a contract which enables them to evaluate the progress they are making toward an agreed end. It is the collective purpose that most frequently keeps small groups from becoming cliques.

Components of a Model

What then should we be looking for in a model or strategy of youth ministry? Five features should dominate our search—a distinct audience, a point of personal contact, a friendly social network, a system of communicating the truth, and a means of discipleship and leadership development. Without any one of these attributes, the so-called model will be in danger of becoming mere activity for young people that looks a lot like baby-sitting Christian youth. Let's examine the five features more closely.

Who is the target audience for this model of youth ministry?

For the first time in the two-century history of youth ministry, this question must be asked. Previously the answer was simple: Parachurch ministries were trying to reach all the students in their high schools. Church youth ministries were trying to reach the young people in their communities, however those communities were defined. No longer is that answer adequate in most places. Today's adolescents inhabit the same space as their contemporaries but live in different worlds. Schools are fragmented into a plethora of identifiable groups that care little about the social currency traded by peers affiliated with other clusters of young people. The activities that interest one group or network of groups is viewed as boring or dumb by another group. One model no longer fits all youth. Perhaps it never did.

For the past twenty-five years, the major parachurch ministries and outreach-oriented church youth groups have competed with each other for the same high school students: college-bound, achievement-oriented youth. Unknowingly, we overlooked as much as 40 percent of the high school population who did not fit the assumed profile of our target audience. In urban and transitional communities, the percentage was much higher.

With the fragmentation of social groupings today, those responding to our ministries is closer to 25 percent of the high school population. In the European community and in some portions of the United States, Canada, and the Commonwealth, the actual audience is probably less than 5 percent of the adolescent population.

In order to establish new directions in youth ministry, the youth minister of the twenty-first century will need to stop broadcasting (trying to reach everyone) and begin narrowcasting (trying to reach specific people groups within the adolescent population). Missionaries have been doing this for years as they have entered new cultures. Youth ministers need to come to grips with the fact that youth ministry, more than ever before, has become a cross-cultural endeavor. Principles of missionology need to be applied to the models of youth ministry that we are creating.

What is our point of contact with the young people we wish to reach?

Youth ministry begins when a Christian finds a mutually comfortable way to enter a young person's world. Ministry starts with a relationship. The youth ministry models of the later twentieth century have, for the most part, been "come" models, in which students have brought peers to Christian adult-sponsored activities. Youth workers then build integrity relationships with the pre-faith students. Clubs and youth group gatherings are the most common examples. This "come" point of contact has worked exceedingly well in many places with many seekers finding in their new teenage and adult friends an integrity that eventually earns a hearing for the gospel.

Unfortunately, it has long been known that the students from our youth groups have a pattern of inviting people who share their values. Athletes invite athletes and wanna-be athletes. Computer nerds invite computer nerds. Hispanics invite Hispanics. Weekend partyers invite weekend partyers. Of course, there are exceptions, but the pattern is fairly clear. Though all youth groups "tolerate" small minorities who have values distinctly different from the group, by and large outsiders would see the kids in each group as very much alike.

One exception should be noted. Certain groups, usually attended by thirty or fewer young people and who have adult leadership which is *aggressively inclusive,* will consist of three or more dissimilar groupings, all of which feel at home and contribute to the spiritual development of the group. My experience suggests that this unique adult leader, while being spiritually and socially mature, frequently appears to be a "burnout" or a nerd. Some other, more average-appearing leaders have gained with patience a reputation on the streets for their openness to and friendship with losers and "ordinary" adolescents. Inclusiveness tends to arise from social weakness rather than from charismatic strength.

The new models of youth ministry are missionary efforts. They will not attract a cross section of the high school society. Contact will need to be made with clusters or networks of students who otherwise would have nothing to do with the church or parachurch ministry. Most youth ministers are so busy shepherding the flock God has given to them that little time is left for such contact work. There are two viable options for establishing contact with new populations of young people. Either a youth minister can empower volunteers to shepherd the youth group and shift a majority (but not all) of his or her time to establishing contact with these new target groups, or he or she can find volunteers uniquely gifted as missionaries and provide them with the resources, authority, and encouragement to *operate outside the lines* in order to minister to a distinct social grouping that may have little or no contact with the existing youth ministry. In fact, the two groups may meet only in the church worship service or at camp.

The point of contact will probably not be in a church building. It may be in a mall, a recreation center, a neighborhood, on campus, or at a workplace. It may happen as a result of common interests (music, skate-boarding, computers, earning money, cars), common problems (dysfunctional families, crime, substance abuse, injustice, academic failure), or unexpected events (fire, death of a peer, personal injury, arrest). In most cases it will not be scheduled conveniently at the normal youth ministry meeting time. Yet it will be from these contacts that new models of youth ministry will develop.

What will earn the right for the Christian message to be presented?

Once contact has been established with a new population of young people, the youth leader must find a way to transition from gospel lived to gospel stated, otherwise no model exists. In a one-on-one relationship, this progression may be rather quick, though not so abrupt as was common at the height of the Jesus Movement of the late sixties. In group settings where ministry models are necessary, the progress from relationship to gospel story is slower.

I would like to propose an hypothesis that should be tested by a doctoral candidate or a religious researcher: Most spiritual growth happens in a manner similar to the way the human body grows, a spurt at a time. Spiritual growth spurts are associated with new ideas, personal crises, or violated relationships. In between growth spurts are periods of solidification in which new spiritual capacities are tested, expanded, and refined.

If this hypothesis is accurate, the responsibility of youth ministry is to ensure that every young person has a spiritually significant relationship with a Christian adult, both when the spurt happens and during the solidification period. When you peel away the layers of organizational structure from the models currently in vogue, each model makes more mature believers of younger believers in a moment of spiritual upheaval. This includes when students first establish a personal relationship with God through Jesus Christ. Competition, discipleship groups, safe places, Christian schools, mission ministries, family models, and meta models all provide contexts in which adult leaders can sustain relationships with small groups of students over an extended period of time with the view of stimulating Christian growth at appropriate times.

Perhaps the most difficult question to answer is, what stimulates spiritual growth? In the past the most common answer was a "loving life" because love was understood to be at the heart of the gospel, even by secular students. Today, however, we cannot make the same assumption. In a pluralistic world, a loving life, while still special, has very little religious connotation. New models of youth ministry will need to provide information about the Christian message in a relational context as a basic way of stimulating spiritual growth.

Motivations for the initial involvement of young people in activities provided by a youth ministry leader are seldom spiritual in nature. Most frequently the motives are social, though many other motivations exist. New models of youth ministry will discover locally appropriate activities that appeal to the targeted young people. These activities will eventually lead to a clear presentation of the Christian gospel.

The models listed in this book are but a few examples of locally appropriate activities that lead to a proclamation of the Christian gospel. Many others will surface in the years ahead. Most will be rather simple. Each reader will find an appropriate activity that appeals to a basic need of a specific group of young people. For those that touch the lives of more than twenty or thirty young people, the model will rely on a growing number of volunteers who will keep the ministry relational and focused.

How will the Christian message be communicated?

More important than any other aspect of the new models is the content and method of communicating the Christian gospel. Though the gospel has not changed, youth culture has. No longer is the gospel convincing to most young people if presented as four points of evidence as in a court of law. We can no longer make basic assumptions about how students understand the nature of God. Perceptions of God are as different as musical tastes or hairstyles. In many cases, youth ministers will have to instruct young people in how to think about the Christian God and the gospel story before asking for a commitment to Christ. More than at any time in the history of Christianity in the Western world, youth culture is more like Athens than Jerusalem. The apostle Paul's strategy in Acts 17 of talking about the "unknown God" is more appropriate for today's young people than the method he used in responding to the Philippian jailer one chapter earlier.

A key component in the Christian apologetic with young people is the emotional confirmation of the message, which is found in the authentic life of a local faith community. While it is still important for an individual friend to live the Christian life, this evidence will not be sufficient. A teenager's Christlike life can be discounted as being unique to that person. Larger groups that demonstrate the gospel lived out in community—especially when they include diversity of age, tastes, and racial background—become a compelling part of the gospel presentation. Students are crying, "Don't tell me, show me."

Authentic beauty may be a third component of the gospel presentation. This generation is looking for more than just pretty faces; it is looking for harmony between the message and the medium of communication. The art, music, video, drama, dance, and speaking styles must be as attractive as the God they profess to represent. Authentic beauty is not to be confused with professional slickness, for while the generation affirms beauty, it abhors synthetic authenticity. Worship music may be the best manifestation of God's beauty.

So how will the Christian gospel be presented in the new models of youth ministry? That may be the most difficult question answered by the creators of innovative strategies.

How will new believers be discipled and use their gifts to do ministry?

One of the keys to new models of ministry is continuity of nurturing relationships. The pattern will be the family rather than the school. Instead of passing kids along from one youth worker to another, determined by age or grade in school, the dynamics of the new discipleship will provide care similar to a large, extended family where older children, grandparents, and even uncles, aunts, and cousins are vital to raising a normal family. Discipleship will take place in small communities or clusters of believers over extended periods of time.

Mark records, "Jesus went up on a mountainside and called to him those he wanted, and they came to him. He appointed twelve—designating them apostles—that they might be with him" (Mark 3:13-14a). Teaching was a byproduct of "being with." Mission was an outgrowth of "being with." Spiritual maturation was associated with "being with." In our attempts to cope with modern society, "learning" has been substituted for "being with" But both are needed for Christian discipleship.

The discipleship aspect of most current youth ministry models is based on a schooling model of training. Specialized teachers, training manuals, graduated curricular materials, group or classroom settings, and segregated age groups characterize the process of nurturing adolescent believers. Youth pastors or club leaders (in formal education they are called teachers) are the experts in this spiritual task. Parents, adult friends, siblings, and assorted other relatives are usually excluded from the process.

Schooling strategies have benefits. They have been useful in raising the standards for discipleship. Published materials allow leaders with good hearts but minimal biblical and theological exposure to shape young Christian minds. The greatest problem in the schooling model of Christian nurture is the lack of continuity of relationships. Three or four hours of weekly contact over the life of an average high schooler's matriculation simply does not satisfy the "being with" principle. It does not appear that the current generation of young people will be "schooled" to maturity in Christ. Something new is needed.

At the heart of continuing relationships is the local church. The only cradle-to-grave social groupings today are the family and the church. Many families are dysfunctional. Others simply dissolve in divorce or death. The faith community, embodied in the local church, has the best chance of providing continuity discipleship through the high school years *and beyond*. The energy of new models of youth ministry will find a way to allow the faith community to be at the heart of adolescent discipleship.

Conclusion

Since all youth ministry is local, what is the point of a book such as this? The answer is simple—*empowerment!* If the authors in this book can create new models of youth ministry, others can too. This is not to suggest the work will be simple, but it can be done.

After four years in youth ministry in my first church and after accepting a call to Arlington Heights Evangelical Free Church, I sat down and evaluated what had worked and what had not worked in my ministry. Looking at the new church, community, and youth group, I became convinced that what I had been doing would not work in the new context. Some new model was needed, but what?

One class I had taken at the University of Illinois, Chicago Circle focused on group communication and process. At the same time, I had been reading about spiritual gifts and wondering how young people could discover and use theirs. Sitting in a library, an idea occurred to me. Why not put these two ideas together? I wrote some ideas in the flyleaf of a textbook, and a ministry model was born.

Within six months I had set up a series of challenging projects in which young people could serve other people and at the same time discover their giftedness for ministry. For the next four years, this gift-development model was at the heart of our youth ministry. Other youth pastors adapted the model to their church situations. A model of ministry was maturing.

Although I know of no one who is currently using the gift-development model of youth ministry, that's OK! Ministry models grow out of local conditions and are effective only as long as the local leadership responds to local needs for ministry.

The challenge before the reader of this book is not so much how you can adopt the models in this book to your local ministry, but how you can respond to the spiritual needs of a specific group of young people and create a strategy for assisting their growth to spiritual maturity in Jesus Christ.

ENDNOTES

1. Richard Dunn and Mark H. Senter III, *Reaching a Generation for Christ* (Chicago: Moody Press, 1997); Warren S. Benson and Mark H. Senter III, *The Complete Book of Youth Ministry* (Chicago: Moody Press, 1987); Warren S. Benson and Roy S. Zuck, *Youth Education in the Church* (Chicago: Moody Press, 1978).

CHAPTER 1:
Platoons and Shepherds

Ministering Through Student-Led Cell Groups

JOHN RUHLMAN

High School Pastor at Shadow Mountain Community Church in El Cajon, California

Where It All Began

It was 6:55 on a mid-October Wednesday evening. Hundreds of students were packed into our newly painted youth room where a huge neon sign blazed "Breakaway." It was weekly outreach night.

Jeremy was tapping my right shoulder, while Megan (surrounded by her four friends) was telling me that Tara was off the deep end with drugs. Our tech team was late setting up the video projector, and the audio wasn't working (and my message was supposed to begin with a video discussion curriculum). Tony, the worship leader, interrupted to tell me that the rest of the band wasn't going to be there—so it was just him.

Jeremy tapped my shoulder again and asked me about summer camp (remember, it was October). I thought to myself, "Where are our volunteers?" Then without warning, I reached my limit. "Jeremy, don't you think there's a better time to talk about summer camp than two minutes before we start Breakaway and ten months before we leave?" I barked. "Sit down, and let's get started." Although I was visibly agitated, my words were barely audible above the roar of what had become teenager social hour. Megan and her friends sheepishly left and found a spot on the floor, whispering about how surly their youth pastor had become.

Frustration had set in—and dissatisfaction too. On the surface, Breakaway night at Shadow Mountain Community Church was blessed. We had excellent facilities and dozens of quality students, some who had been discipled for years. Many teenagers brought friends. We had experienced an explosion in numbers.

By all outward appearances, God was doing a work that was unprecedented in suburban San Diego. Parking and crowd control were weekly issues. Students were placing their faith in Christ—by the dozens. Parents, pastors, deacons, and elders were enthralled with the high energy and the number of students in our youth ministry program. This was the traditional youth pastor's dream. I was overwhelmed with pats on the back, accolades, and thank you notes.

So were we reaching our goals? Simply stated, our mission was (and still is) "to turn high school students into fully devoted followers of Christ." Our mission was clear, biblical, and honorable. But when we honestly looked at the results of our traditional model of youth ministry...ouch. Mission failure: students slipping through as fast as they'd come, surface-level spirituality with rare depth. It was clear that we needed to rework our model.

Early Failures

Two years earlier we had come to a similar conclusion. A fully honest assessment at the time had revealed that we weren't fulfilling the Great Commission. We prayed and studied God's Word and concluded that we were missing the "discipleship" element that Christ had modeled.

We started care groups. We spent many hours recruiting and training our adult staff to disciple small groups. After we launched them—as a supplement to Breakaway and Sunday school—we were sure we had a biblical model of what youth ministry should be. Our preparation had been meticulous: We had prayed, prepared, and assigned the students to perfect little platoons. We had even tried to keep friends together. No one would slip through the cracks.

Care groups failed. Based on our goals, we had prayed that God would increase the number of students being discipled through the care groups. Well, after three months we had lost over one-third of our adult staff. They didn't all say they were quitting volunteer ministry; many just sort of phased themselves out due to a feeling of nonaccomplishment. Most sincere-hearted adults just weren't connecting with the teenagers.

These adults had made a noble effort, but I had set them up for failure. I had given each one a list of twenty students. After they had spent hours on the phone, in training, and in prayer, most had three or four students show up for the first few weeks of care group. Eventually the three or four tapered off to one or two—with even the committed and responsible students calling their group leaders to say, "I've got too much homework tonight, but I'll probably be there next week."

While the care groups were falling apart, Breakaway was still thriving. It was meeting the social needs the students weren't getting met elsewhere. I had two questions at that point:

● Is God still calling me to be in youth ministry?

● Where, if anywhere, are these teenagers becoming fully devoted followers of Christ? If it was at Breakaway or in care groups, it was marginal at best.

The phone calls began to trickle in. Some were honest: "Maybe God hasn't called me to be a youth volunteer through discipling a small group. I've given it my best, and the students just have too much going on to be in a small group." Some weren't quite as honest: "Thanks so much for the opportunity to serve in youth ministry, but my boss has just changed my hours, and I don't think that I'm going to be able to keep working with my care group."

I felt like the steward of a huge, mature, and beautiful orchard. We spent enormous energy watering, fertilizing, and weeding the grove. Yet the trees bore small fruit—some very healthy trees of good "Christian lineage" yielded nothing. It seemed impossible to spend personal time pruning every individual tree. The trees were too numerous and the farmhands too few. Besides, by my experience, no matter how much I trained the farmhands, most of them failed at pruning, watering, and weeding anyway.

Back to the Blowup

At home after Breakaway that evening, I shared with my wife how I had unloaded on Jeremy. My outburst had surprised me, and I was plagued with guilt. My passion was to share with students the same life-changing message that had brought me out of despair. My intentions were right, but the method needed reworking.

How could this method be wrong? After all, this entertainment "magnet" model was the same model of "youth group" that I had grown up in. It was the model I had learned in Bible college. It was used across America. Wasn't it in some way based on the Bible? Didn't Christ speak to the multitudes?

But after years of using this "rah-rah" model, there were evenings when I was backstage ready to give my talk to more than three hundred teenagers, and a feeling of dread would come over me. It was a deep longing to see true spiritual growth in young people. I began to understand that if students came to be entertained, they would go home just that—entertained.

A New Idea

I began to reflect on the process God had used to call me to youth ministry. As a high school history teacher fresh out of college, I was baffled by the extraordinary leadership skills and accomplishments of the students at that Christian high school. These kids had the Holy Spirit's power. Their hearts for missions and service were authentic. I had watched fifteen of the students from my advanced-placement European history class sharing their faith on the streets of Bratislava, Slovakia.

I came to realize that although a teenager is still growing and learning, the Holy Spirit who indwells these students *is not a child*. That was it—entrusting students to take a more active role in the small group model. God began to rework my entire thought process. What if we encourage mature, Christlike student leaders to use the gifts God has given them, and commission each one to have an active role in the ministry. These kids could be the "platoon leaders."[1]

When I shared my passion about platoons with my senior pastor, he gave me his full support. I shared with my staff the idea of student-led and adult-coached discipleship ministry. I could barely contain my excitement. My animated speech at our monthly staff meeting was met with rolling eyes, smiles, and deep sighs. Although our staff of dedicated leaders was supportive, they had been through our attempts at small-group ministry before. However, their interest was sharpened when I declared my desire to stop holding the weekly entertainment-based Breakaway and to hold platoons in its place.

Three months later, we punted on the long-standing Breakaway. This midweek teenage meeting had met for more than fifty years (under various names) at our church. I expected our numbers to plummet from more than two hundred to forty or fifty. I was determined that it was worth it—we could start with a core of committed kids and build as the original eleven had in the New Testament church.

God proved that he was in control. In the first year of platoons, our numbers increased! But numbers weren't what made it worthwhile. It was the personal attention each student was getting. "Every student with a shepherd" was our goal. Now we were closer to this goal than ever before.

God took a student ministry in San Diego and made it his ministry. He took it from a large group of teenagers who were attending for the wrong reasons—and he transformed many of their lives. He multiplied their slow spiritual growth while multiplying their numbers. Early tremors of a revival have been shaking through these obedient students' lives. Teenagers are getting personal attention and discipleship in small groups. It's amazing to see a plant grow—especially when you thought it was dead!

For those of you whose philosophy is "We count people because people count," here are some numbers: Shadow Mountain's student ministry grew numerically by nearly 50 percent in the first year and over 100 percent in the past four years. Shadow Mountain currently has forty-eight student-led cell groups, ministering to the personal needs of individual students in an almost eighty-mile radius of our church. But the real explosion has been in spiritual growth. You can't put a measuring stick on spiritual growth. You can only thank God for the incredible things he does.

Same Seed, Different Soil

One evening as I pulled the church bus into the parking lot after SNIFF (Sunday Night in Fun and Fellowship), I was surprised to see a patrol car waiting with the parents. As I stepped off the bus, the officer approached and said, "Are you Pastor Ruhlman? There's been a shooting at your home, and you're wanted at the police station immediately."

My body weakened as she told me a man had climbed the fence of my back yard and pried open the only window that had a direct view of my wife (three months pregnant at the time) and my two-year-old daughter. Carrie and Rachel were in bed watching TV. When my wife saw a figure crawl through the window across the hall, she called out, "John...is that you?" Realizing it wasn't me, she sprang from the bed to protect herself and her children. Quickly she grabbed the gun from the top of the bureau and warned the intruder, "Stop! I have a gun!" With that, the intruder lunged at her. My wife shot him through the lung at point-blank range. Although my family will never be the same, God healed the intruder, and he's now working his way through the criminal justice system.

As I reflected on this event, three things came to mind:

- God protects his own.
- My house won't get toilet-papered for a long time.
- Our society has changed.

Today's teenagers are growing up in a different world. They're the same flesh and blood we were as teenagers, but the soil they're planted in is very different. Teenage crime has run rampant. Sex, drugs, violent and nonviolent crime, free choice, and humanistic teaching are everywhere. *If we fail to adapt our methods to reach these teenagers where they are, we will fail to reach them.* But fertile soil comes from death and decomposition. This is the soil our nation's young people are planted in. This is the kind of soil from which awakenings emerge!

Trickledown Philosophy[2]

One dominant strategy of youth ministry for the past fifty years has been to reach the leaders in the high school and encourage them in turn to reach the rest of the high school. The philosophy was simple and effective: Go to the high school, and target the student-body president, the captain of the football team, and the captain of the cheerleading squad as your leaders. If the most popular kids come, the effect will "trickle down" and most of the other students will want to be there. Throw a "burger bash," and eventually form a club to reach teenagers through lots of fun events and relational evangelism.

This model worked for a while, but now it's like trying to plant a palm tree in the frozen tundra of Nome, Alaska. And we're all scratching our heads wondering why it's not growing. The soil is different. The motive is right, but the method must change.

Today's High School Society: Fragmented

If you ask a student in one of today's high schools who the student-body president, captain of the football team, and cheerleading captain are, they probably won't know and don't care.

The high schools of this nation are fragmented societies. Teenagers are divided into groups and have very little in common with those outside their own groups. With this fragmentation of youth culture, the church must rethink its youth ministry strategy.

This is why student-led cell groups make sense. The "skater" boys meet together in a platoon group led by a skater boy who's excited about Christ. Sound too much like a clique? Cliques are a fact. Teenage society fragmentation is a fact. Cliques pose a problem only if the cliques are closed. In other words, Joey's skater platoon must keep an empty chair open for other skaters who need to know Christ.

Knowing Your Targets

Youth ministers around the world have three types of teenagers in their ministries: the student leaders, the believers, and the seekers. We could name dozens of programs that minister to the student leader, dozens that minister to the believer, and dozens of "outreach programs" that minister to the seeker.

Nearly every church tries to perpetuate three or more programs for these three categories of teenagers. Churches have an arsenal of weapons, yet they haven't mastered any. The youth staff is overwhelmed with "programs." Adults are worn out. Teenagers are worn out. *The youth pastor is worn out.*

Student-led cell groups hit all three target student groups.

● LEADERS become doers of the faith, not just hearers (James 2:14-26). They become disciple makers (Matthew 28:19) and fill their toolboxes with skills for college and beyond. All the while, that student leader is being personally discipled by a caring, Christlike adult "coach."

● BELIEVERS grow, receive discipleship, are cared for, and get individual attention. These students can develop into student leaders.

● SEEKERS fill the "empty chair." They feel welcome, are loved, and can't slip through the cracks. They come for lasting personal relationships, not entertainment.

Where It All Started

Platoon groups are not a new idea. They're rooted in the two-thousand-year-old model that Christ used to minister on earth. He chose twelve, graduated eleven, failed one, focused on three (Peter, James, and John); and according to the biblical record, spent most of his time with one—John. Those eleven disciples—empowered with the same Holy Spirit we have—turned the world upside down for Christ.

What if we, as youth leaders, used Jesus' model? What if we were to spend the majority of our time with the "Johns" of our ministry? What if we were disciple makers? What if we invested and equipped our student leaders to disciple others—then put a handle on the package and let these students pick it up? The church typically equips, equips, equips, yet fails to truly entrust these teenagers with discipling others. What a wasted resource.

Christ didn't call us in Matthew 28:19 to "make converts." Conversion is only half the process. He commissioned us to *make disciples*. *Disciple makers make disciple makers who make disciple makers.* That's the foundation of student-led cell groups. They're biblical. They're explosive.

How Does It Work?

Some Definitions

PLATOON—a student-led cell group

PLATOON LEADER—the student leader

PLATOON APPRENTICE—the student leader in training

PLATOON COACH—the adult mentor of the platoon leader and apprentice

DIVISION DIRECTOR—the "shepherd of shepherds" who oversees, encourages, and trains the coaches and student leaders within the division

The Keys to Coaching

● The platoon coach must meet with the platoon leader and the apprentice once a week outside the platoon meeting for discipleship and mentoring.

● The platoon coach must attend all platoon meetings and activities.

The Platoon Meeting

TIME—usually an hour and a half

DAY—any evening, usually Monday through Thursday

PLACE—in a home, usually of the platoon leader, apprentice, or coach

CURRICULUM—The youth minister may decide on the Bible study or may delegate the decision to the platoon coach and platoon leader. The choice should be based on the "spiritual climate" of those attending the platoon.

Platoon Meeting Agenda

There are five necessary elements in each platoon meeting.

● FRESH BREAD—"God is baking some bread in your oven. Someone share some piping-hot fresh bread." Here is where the Word comes alive in a student's life. It's where personal study is applied to life circumstances and shared with the group. Students share passages of Scripture and why those passages impacted their lives during the week.[3]

● ANNOUNCEMENTS—Mundane as it may sound, this is an effective tool that ties all the platoons together as one body. It also ties the youth ministry to congregational events and activities. The announcement sheet is produced weekly by the youth minister's office. It's distributed to the coaches and platoon leaders.

● PRAYER SHARE AND CARE—This is a time for students to share prayer requests and care for each other. Prayer requests are journaled, and each student is cared for. In a group of ten or less, no one falls through the cracks.

● BIBLE STUDY—The platoon leader facilitates the study. On rare occasions the coach leads. Eventually the platoon leader and apprentice can develop the tools to effectively teach the Word. The coach steps in when "touchy" doctrinal issues come up and is trained to challenge the students to study God's Word for themselves.

● EMPTY CHAIR—Students always leave the best chair in the room open. They take the time to name the people they know who need Christ or need to be cared for, and they pray for these students by name. When these "prayed-for" students attend, they're genuinely welcomed and given the best seat in the house. The empty chair eclipses the problem of new students feeling left out.

Grouping Students

It's important to realize that our fragmented society has crushed the old Sunday school model of dividing teenagers into gender- and age-oriented groups. Different students have different interests and maturity levels. They hang out with each other across grade levels and even schools.

Student-led cell groupings are based wholly on the relationships the platoon leader and coach already have established (and will establish). For example, if Becky, a platoon leader, plays volleyball at one of the local high schools, her platoon will consist of those she cares about and spends the most time with—probably including some members of the volleyball team. It's the same scenario with Steve who plays in the marching band. His band buddies are his most likely targets as members of his platoon. Joe, who is into computers, will invite, care for, and encourage computer fans. Jack, who is a linebacker on the football team, will have a living room full of hungry gridiron warriors—every one of which needs to be cared for.

Components of the Model

Of course a student-led cell group ministry can be adapted to your own ministry and schedule of events. We've learned, though, that this schedule fits best for us.

SUMMER—an important sabbatical from platoons. This time off gives a defined break from the weekly small group that meets throughout the school year.

LEADERSHIP RETREATS—an important training- and community-building tool. It's critical to teach the fundamental tools of discipleship here. The time includes both fun activities and targeted training. The purpose is twofold:

● Day 1: Personal renewal—We can't teach others to seek Christ if we're not committed to seeking him.

● Days 2 and 3: Leadership training—Practical workshops designed to give student leaders and staff practical tools for leading small groups. Seminar topics can be delegated to your interns, pastors, or capable volunteers.

We hold two leadership retreats every year, one in August as a kick-off (the week before fall athletics begin) and one in December. The second retreat comes after Christmas and before the new year. It provides student leadership with a "recharge" to commence the second semester of platoons.

MONTHLY TRAINING—a follow-up training time for student leaders and staff. This time is a combination of worship, encouragement, biblical teaching, sharing blessings, and praying for challenges.

TARGET NIGHTS—once-a-month outreach nights for every student in every platoon to "target" non-Christian friends. Target night is a fun, activity-oriented evening where we present a gospel message. Students are given a chance to respond to this message. Students who commit their lives to Christ have their "new believers" class already in place—platoons. The same students who invited them to target night invite them to their own platoons. The relationship is already there, and the platoon has been praying for this teenager to fill that empty chair.

BIRTHING PROCESS—When a platoon reaches a steady twelve members or more, half the group goes with the apprentice to help "birth" a new platoon. Half stays with the original platoon leader. Students choose who to go with. Of course a new coach must be recruited to disciple the new group.

SNIFF—Sunday Night in Fun and Fellowship is a community-building event following the evening service in the Big House (the church). The purpose is twofold—it encourages students to attend the evening teaching time with our senior pastor while providing a place where students can connect afterward. From week to week, we rotate between "fun activities" and more "worshipful" settings.

Choosing Your Student Leaders

You probably already know who many of your student leaders are, but here are two basic characteristics to look for.

● GENUINE EXCITEMENT AND GROWTH IN THEIR RELATIONSHIP WITH CHRIST—These kids' talk should match their walk at school, at work, in their relationships, and on the athletic field.

● LEADERSHIP ABILITY—If they lead, who will follow? I learned the hard way that some of my best student leaders aren't the loud, popular, answer-all-the-questions-type students.

Building and Training a Student Leadership Team

If you want to develop training materials on your own, do so by focusing on your students' areas of need. Enlist your volunteer staff to lead seminars during your leadership retreats. As your small groups develop, you'll become aware of the critical areas of need for instruction.

If you don't want to develop your own materials, there are several training resources available. Check out Group Publishing's *Training Youth for Dynamic Leadership*. Shadow Mountain Student Ministries also offers a training manual, a computer disk, and an audiocassette tape series.

How God Is Using the Student-Led Cell Groups

NAELLI RODREGUEZ—"But Pastor John, I liked the closeness we used to have in our ministry before it grew. I wish we could stay small in our 'bigness.' " Naelli's Spanish accent broke through clearly at our first leadership retreat's Where Do We Go From Here? seminar. Her comment met with the approval of the other student leaders. The students themselves saw the need for small groups.

JAKE SMITH—"John, can I please lead a platoon? I know I can do it. I know God is calling me." I winced as I thought of the prospect. Due to his shaky social skills and different appearance, his peers continuously mocked Jake. I was convinced we would be setting him up for failure.

I tried to choose my words carefully to discourage the process. "Jake, why don't you apprentice a platoon this year and gain some insight and maturity for the leadership process?" But he was persistent. Finally I conceded, "Here's the deal, Jake. If you give me the names and phone numbers of seven students who commit to your platoon, you can come on our leadership retreat." Not three days later, Jake gave me ten names.

Still not convinced, I struggled to find a coach for Jake. Finally a young, Christlike United States Marine joined our staff and saw the hunger Jake had. They kicked off their platoon. No one came. Three weeks later, still no one was there but Jake and Doug, his coach. They began to see their meetings as great discipleship time. Two months and more than thirty invitations later...still no one had come. Then, in the ninth week of the semester, two local high school students who had never been to church showed up. Then four students came, then six. Today, as a senior, Jake still gets teased — but God has used him over the last three years to minister to dozens of students. Just last night Jake ministered to nine students at the platoon in his home.

DOROTHY BECKER—Yesterday's e-mail came from George Washington University in Washington, D.C. It read, "John, I miss my family and my platoon so much, but God has led me to a great church here, and I'm meeting with a group of students in my dorm each week for our own little platoon." Dorothy made a commitment to Christ two years ago. Her platoon had reached a previously untouched population in one of the farthest schools in our district last year. It continues this year with her apprentice as the platoon leader.

TIM KUHL—Tim showed up at a youth beach event one day in the spring of his junior year. He hadn't been to church for years, except for Easter and Christmas. Tim was like a magnet to other students. He was humble and handsome. That month he was elected student-body president. He was the captain of his football team. But Tim's success hadn't gone to his head. That summer he grew spiritually and was discipled. In the fall, he led an incredible platoon. Today Tim is a youth pastor.

JACKIE CAREY—In the previous three years, I had known Jackie's face, but I could barely attach her name to her face. She didn't talk. She was always there, but she blended easily into the crowd. But Jackie was excited about her relationship with Christ. As our staff gathered to pray and choose our leadership team, one of our interns mentioned Jackie as a candidate for platoon leadership. Only a few knew who she was. Last year Jackie's platoon ministered to a sixteen-year-old girl who had become pregnant. The girls threw her a shower, encouraged her weekly at the platoon, prayed for her, discipled her, and introduced her to Jesus. Jackie ministers to a group of girls who would have never darkened the door of a church.

DAVE MILLER—Dave's an incredible young man, excited about Jesus. Dave is a disciple maker. For three years he led a platoon that has birthed eleven other platoons. Each one is led by a teenager that Dave discipled over the years. Dave is currently on our youth staff, encouraging and equipping nine of Dave's newly birthed platoons. Five other students from Dave's high school platoon are currently on our youth staff coaching platoons.

JENNY GILIO—Jenny Gilio lives on a beautiful resort island on the west side of San Diego Harbor. This affluent community struggles with a teenage population that has all the niceties of life. Jenny couldn't make the weekly forty-minute drive to our area for a midweek program. So she began a platoon that helped teenagers in her area deal with their unique, difficult issues.

Possible Pitfalls

● THE ADD-ON PIT—One of the common mistakes ministries make is adding platoons to their current entertainment-based model. We're a student ministry of cell groups, not a student ministry with cell groups. We funnel everything we do through this filter: "Will it assist or build up the platoons?"

● THE I-WANT-TO-RUN-IT-ALL MINISTRY MIND-SET—Pride has no place in ministry, especially student-led cell ministry. Youth ministers must be able to step back and allow the students to lead.

● INSUFFICIENT SHEPHERDING OF COACHES—Youth ministers must equip and encourage leadership in others.

● INSUFFICIENT DISCIPLING/MENTORING OF PLATOON LEADERS AND AP-
PRENTICES—Equipping teenagers to lead other teenagers is discipleship.
As important as the platoon itself is the time spent with student leaders. The "coaching" sessions the day before the platoon meeting are
where disciple making begins.

● WRONG SELECTION OF STUDENT LEADERSHIP—Don't take just anyone—only those who meet your rigid criteria. Here's a suggestion that has
been effective for us: Of those selected, only the ones who complete a de-
tailed application and submit two written references are considered. This
filters out the students who feel honored to be chosen but have too much
going on to be fully committed.

● FORCING GENDER-EXCLUSIVE GROUPS—Teenagers will open up far
more to teenagers of their own sex. But some groups will be as or more
effective with both boys and girls. One of our young married couples decided to coach a platoon that consisted of dating couples. It was a great
platoon, but the turnover rate was terribly high. Actually dozens of the
small groups voluntarily decided to limit themselves to guys or girls only
because they saw the value in discussing more intimate issues.

● FORCING CURRICULUM—Although it's a good idea to have a unified curriculum for the first month, soon the student leaders and staff
will see a specific need in the group.

● FORCING MEETING DAY—When we began platoons, it seemed obvious that since we did Breakaway on Wednesday night, we'd do platoons on the same night. Some of our best student leaders came to me
and said, "Pastor John, I work on Wednesday night. I guess I can't lead
a platoon." I checked the Bible and couldn't find the Wednesday-only
mandate. Now our platoons meet Monday through Thursday evenings.
We even have a few that meet Sunday afternoons.

● ALLOWING TRANSIENT PLATOONS—Once in a while it's OK for a
platoon to meet at a new venue, but there's much confusion if all the
phone calls aren't made.

Applying the Model

Ministry to teenagers isn't passive. It must have clear purpose and
direction. We must continually evaluate the effectiveness of the tools
God has given us in order to do our best for him. Remember, the ministry is his, not yours.

The following key elements should be present in order for a student-led cell model to work most effectively:

● your senior pastor's and church leadership's support,

- a youth ministry of ten or more active students,
- tender hearts toward God's leading,
- students who need to put faith in action,
- prayer,
- vision,
- leadership,
- a core of students who have had some level of discipleship,
- a few committed volunteer staff members,
- homes to meet in, and
- some students who need to be encouraged to open up and talk about real issues.

The Junior High Factor

Most of our nation's youth groups include a combination of junior and senior high students. So how do junior high students fit into the student-led cell group model? There are a number of ways to integrate junior high discipleship. All of them require intensive relationship building. Here are a few suggestions:

- The majority of student ministries don't have the luxury of separating junior and senior high students. Not to worry. This provides a unique opportunity for spiritually mature older teenagers to disciple the younger adolescents. It's a model that can produce tangible spiritual growth. When proper training and leadership emerge from your selected senior high platoon leadership, junior highers gain the consistent personal attention they rarely would have experienced before. It also gives the younger students something to strive for.

- If you're fortunate to have enough staff to keep the groups separate, a small-group format during your midweek program can be integrated into your junior high ministry. But because junior highers can't drive, it usually isn't feasible to meet in homes. We've found it most effective to combine a rally format with small groups for junior highers. After a rally you can divide the early adolescents into common-interest or friendship groups who meet in classrooms or outdoors. Student leaders should take on more limited responsibilities.

Closing Thoughts

God has called you to minister to teenagers. You've devoted a great portion of your existence to sharing the good news with these impressionable young people. God will make good on his promise to you: "He who began a good work in you will carry it on to completion" (Philippians 1:6b).

For the twenty-first century, it's clear that God is creating student ministry models to help students, families, and churches connect with God and each other. All over the world, many of these models have one thing in common: They're ministries of small groups modeled after Jesus' ministry.

Because the movement in youth ministry of student-led, adult-coached small groups is still growing, we're all learning from each other. This chapter is not a finished product! Our ministry model will adapt and grow with each new generation. God help us if we stop growing and learning and start assuming we have all the answers!

Those of us in the high school ministry at Shadow Mountain Community Church would like to thank and acknowledge the following people who have given us permission to glean inspiration, insight, knowledge, encouragement, and materials: Dr. David Jeremiah, Ray Benton, Marvin Jacobo, Ted Stump, Wayne Rice, Bo Boshers, Mark Senter, Phil Payne, Carrie Ruhlman, Kaylene Jeffers, John J. Ruhlman Sr., and many others.

ENDNOTES

1. The term "platoons" comes from the sermon "Enlisting in Little Platoons," by Bill Hybels.

2. Mark H. Senter III, from the seminar "The Essential Paradigm Shift in Youth Ministry," October 28, 1996.

3. The concept of "fresh bread" came from Phil Payne at Community Baptist Church in Lake Arrowhead, California.

CHAPTER 2:
An Oasis of Hope

A Working Model for Urban Ministry

HARVEY F. CAREY
Youth Pastor at Salem Baptist Church of Chicago in Chicago, Illinois

Urban youth ministry wears many faces. Whether in the main town of a somewhat rural community or in the middle of a major metropolis, teenagers in many settings are considered "urban." As you read this chapter, don't confuse urban youth ministry with inner city youth ministry. The backdrop for this particular model happens to be inner city urban youth ministry. However, the two terms are quite different. The inner city is housed within the urban setting, but all urban ministry is not necessarily inner city ministry.

Salem Baptist Church of Chicago serves as home base for this youth ministry program. Located in the middle of one of the poorest regions on the south side of Chicago, this church has experienced phenomenal growth. Through strong biblical teaching and loving outreach to the community, we've grown to become one of the largest churches in Chicago. The youth ministry has found inroads into the community and surrounding areas by taking the biblical principles of Christ and an understanding of the needs of urban young people and conducting explosive ministry within that context. Understanding the urban teenager and the special needs a church in that setting is called to address will be the highlights of this chapter. In the paragraphs to follow, you can expect to read and be inspired, enlightened, and equipped to minister to urban teenagers.

The urban Chicagoland region of Roseland is an area defined by crime, unemployment, drug use, gang violence, low academic test scores, and hopelessness. In this setting Salem Baptist Church of Chicago invested in hiring me as full-time youth pastor to oversee its ministry to teenagers. At the time, there were few teenagers in the youth ministry, and they were primarily the children of adults in our church. I felt ill-equipped (although I had undergraduate training in religious studies and youth ministry) to meet the needs of inner city teenagers. I felt as if the challenge was too great and my database too empty.

Eight Track vs. Compact Disc

An eight-track cassette player and a CD player both serve the same purpose: playing music. But the eight track doesn't have the clarity of the original recording and doesn't allow people to access songs with great speed. Eight tracks are also cumbersome. CDs, on the other hand, provide studio-quality sound, allow us to program songs to repeat or to play in a certain order, and are very easy to carry.

The church has a timeless, endless message to share—Jesus Christ as our only mediator to God. However, many churches are using eight-track methods in a CD generation. The message doesn't have to change, but the church must develop creative, innovative new methods.

Need-Based Ministry

Webster's dictionary defines "ministry" as the "filling of wants." This isn't far from the biblical example defined by Christ as he ministered to people. Jesus met physical, social, and spiritual needs. As we look at urban youth ministry, we must then be concerned about determining and meeting the needs of urban young people. Since our perception of their needs and their actual needs could be far from the same, the process of evaluation is vital.

During the first few months of our ministry, we took regular walks through the community and schools, finding out the needs of the young people in the area of our church. Urban teenagers are often suspicious of people coming to "give" them something or "help" them, and written surveys can be intimidating. So we opted to take mental notes as we asked pointed questions about what hurt them about the community, what they felt the church could really do to make their lives better, and what they wished they could do as teenagers. Once we saw some consistent patterns of need, we knew what type of ministry to conduct.

I can't stress enough the importance of this step in preparing programs. In addition to asking questions, visit the local music store and pick up the top album among urban youth to put your finger on the pulse of the emotions, values, and thoughts of these teenagers. Visit a local newsstand; countless magazines feature trends among urban young people.

The ministry of Christ is as alive as it has always been. We carry his active power, ready to be unleashed on a generation of urban young people who are in search of someone real and powerful. Since we have such a powerful treasure, urban youth ministry programs are agents of the very power of the living God. Each program or event we plan is actually the way we enable God's power to flow to the life of the urban teenager.

Because of the varied and unique gifts in the urban environment, the youth leader in this setting will have no problem finding a vibrant expression of Christ to share with other believers. The only obstacle might be in building self-esteem and motivation in the lives of the teenagers so they choose to dispense the power of God through their gifts.

The Model

Church Within a Church

We adopted the model of the "youth church" within our church. This means we approach the youth ministry as a functioning church within our larger church body. We developed worship, discipleship, preaching, and outreach just as an adult church would approach ministry. With this as our focus, we began with a dozen teenagers in a small chapel on our church campus.

Several key components make the youth church model succeed.

1. EXPOSITORY PREACHING

I opted to teach verse by verse rather than topically so the youth would come to have a great appreciation of the contextual meaning of the Bible. The teenagers have grown to appreciate the Bible and personal study and application. Within the textual study, we address topics such as peer pressure, integrity, and lust. In other words, the topics evolve from the text.

2. STRONG SUNDAY SCHOOL INSTRUCTION

Since Salem believes that the teaching of God's Word is foremost, we've developed the largest Sunday school in Chicago. The youth department of the Sunday school chooses to reinforce the messages I preach by providing in-depth studies of the same texts and related Scriptures. They also tie this teaching into age-appropriate topics for each grade level.

3. SMALL-GROUP DISCIPLESHIP

Although we don't focus heavily on small groups, we do believe young people who are being trained and groomed for leadership should receive specific instruction. The small groups are designed with those student leaders in mind. The instruction is focused on particular areas of leadership.

As we used these methods, the teenagers began to get excited about church. Word began to spread, and our numbers increased.

The Details

This urban youth ministry model consists of three major facets: worship, discipleship, and evangelism.

WORSHIP

As the teenagers develop spiritually, we empower them for Christian service by allowing them to use their gifts within the ministry. We reach young people by sharing the message of Christ clearly. We keep them by allowing them opportunities to participate in ministry through our departments of ministry: rap, stepping, drama, marketing, choral singing, liturgical praise dancing, media, and peer leadership.

● **Rap**—Like any other art form, rap represents a snapshot of the thoughts, feelings, and attitudes of this generation. Many teenagers rap in the corridors and in front of the church. When we ask them what the songs are, they're often too embarrassed to tell us. They struggle because they enjoy rap, but they don't feel as though its application is biblical or correct. We're using rap to share the message of Christ. The Holy Spirit has a tremendous way of taking the same gifts the enemy has perverted and using them to honor God. Rapping has proven to be one of the greatest tools for winning lost teenagers to Christ at Salem. Through rap we've seen literally hundreds of unchurched young people meet Christ.

● **Stepping**—As I prayed and endeavored to find creative ways to express the energy and talent of the young people in our church, we developed our male and female stepping teams. These teams use synchronized steps and hand clapping set to chants that proclaim the awesome power of God.

● **Drama**—Through high school Christian cliffhangers, tear-jerkers, and comedy, the high school theatrical troupe transforms biblical truths into messages that relate to teenagers. Our theatrical troupe speaks in allegorical skits that share the theme and message of the day.

● **Marketing**—Our youth church services are always audiotaped and often videotaped. The teenagers learn methods of reproducing and selling the tapes. And they use their business acumen to effectively market the church's ministry to the youth of Chicago.

● **Choral singing**—Every Sunday our choir sings new songs that energize, encourage, and comfort the teenagers who gather to worship.

● **Liturgical praise dancing**—The praise dancers perform liturgical dance choreographed with a song. Their movements and gestures visually tell the story of the song. These praise dancers provide a visual parable to the teenagers gathering for worship.

● **Media**—We allow teenagers to handle the audiotaping, videotaping, and editing for all our church services. Many young people who don't feel comfortable in upfront ministry fit in perfectly with the media ministry.

● **Peer leadership**—Junior deacons and young women of the altar serve as peer leaders and elders within the youth ministry. Since peer pressure is so common, we disciple these teenagers to be spiritual leaders to their peers. They offer Scripture readings, prayer, and special times of personal counseling. As teenagers flood into the sanctuary, teenage ushers and greeters escort them to their seats and answer general questions about the youth church. They set up chairs and sound equipment, and they clean. Other teenagers see their maturity both in the front of the church during the worship and long before and after the official worship service. Approximately 10 percent of our students have established high school Bible clubs that conduct weekly meetings. Through these Bible clubs, the teenagers from Salem are taking the gospel into their high schools. They truly are examples of the believers.

As the teenagers began to notice their spiritual gifts, they stepped out and became part of the body of Christ and the church in ways that were original and within the context of their unique gifts. The youth ministry began to grow both spiritually and numerically. Each Sunday our worship services—which have a unique urban flair—are filled with life and excitement. We've outgrown the room we were in and moved into the gymnasium.

Hundreds of teenagers gather in this gym-turned-sanctuary to worship, learn, and be sent back into the heart of the urban world to shine the light of Christ. In addition to our worship services and Sunday school, we conduct once-a-month seeker-targeted services called J.A.M. (Jesus and Me) sessions.

DISCIPLESHIP

The majority of discipleship in our program takes place within mentoring relationships. Adult volunteers assigned to teenagers are responsible for finding out their grades, struggles, and victories in the Lord. These volunteers also reinforce the current spiritual emphasis of the youth church. These mentors have built incredible relationships with our young people.

Urban youth ministry involves so much more than programming. Although successful programs are an integral part of any effective youth ministry, they aren't the main force behind powerful urban ministry. Integrity is such a key issue with the fragile emotions of urban youth. The lifestyle of each leader and youth worker is vital to the successful communication of biblical truth.

Although I believe integrity is essential in any ministry, urban youth ministry especially requires it. Urban teenagers have consistently been let down by parents, political officials, teachers, and often society in general. As a result, when they turn to the church, we can't allow inconsistencies to mar the image of Christ. This is why selecting and training urban youth workers is vital.

Adult leaders are a very important part of our ministry model at Salem Baptist Church of Chicago. Indeed, we couldn't do without them. On a weekly basis, we meet with adult leaders of every department within the youth ministry. These lay leaders have been selected from the congregation and have gone through training for Christian youth work.

EVANGELISM

As we do outreach, all our departments come together and use their individual gifts to share the message of Christ. And through Sunday school and our youth church sermons, we work to equip young people to share their faith.

Every month our young people participate in an "evangelism invasion." During these events our teenagers go into the housing projects, drug houses, and streets of Chicago to share the good news of Christ through door-to-door and mass evangelistic worship services. Annually we take this invasion to the most crime-ridden areas of our nation. We've invaded gang-infested, drug-ruled, and poverty-stricken communities in Atlanta, Los Angeles, Little Rock, Dallas, New Haven, and New York.

Simple Methods for Building Your Youth Ministry

This section contains some ideas for building your youth ministry from the ground up. These are simple ideas any church can do.

● LOCK-INS—Of all the events that have brought tremendous success and "mileage" to our youth ministry, lock-ins win the prize hands down. These are by far the greatest events our youth ministry conducts annually. During these all-night sessions, we dispense truth, form relationships, cast vision, uncover gifts, and build self-esteem.

We hold the lock-ins on church premises. Usually we target a specific group of teenagers such as freshmen, choir, or underclassmen guys. Sometimes the groups are handpicked, but often we announce the lock-in during our youth church service and appeal to the group we're trying to target.

The lock-in is of no cost to the teenager. Usually food is as simple as hot dogs, chips, plenty of sodas, and sweets. Although I'm sure health-conscious youth leaders would include yogurt, raisins and the like, I just never have gone that route!

During the lock-in, we hold activities that center around a theme. For example, one lock-in theme was "trust." During the night, we blindfolded the teenagers and led them on a faith walk around the church at one o'clock in the morning. Remember, our church is in the middle of the 'hood. This was a faith walk for real! We followed it up with discussion, a study of Scripture, and more activities including a "faith fall" (falling backward into each other's arms) and relay races in the dark (guided by the words of the peer youth leader in each group).

Lock-ins are as creative as the leaders who plan them. They're inexpensive, and they allow you to recognize the student leaders who are emerging within your particular ministry.

● RETREATS—These times of reflection are life-changing for urban young people. The term "concrete jungle" is often quite accurate. Imagine day after day of concrete, pollution, noise, and—in the inner city urban settings—crime, drugs, and unemployment.

This is the environment many of our young people live in. One can only imagine the toll it takes on a young person who is attempting to give his or her life to the Lord and literally at every turn, faces discouragement, hopelessness, and fear. Imagine never having seen a horse, a farm, or even a rural area at all!

It's with this in mind that we conduct retreats apart from the hustle and bustle of the city and allow these urban young people to enjoy a rural setting. Urban youth ministry should strive to allow its teenagers to be exposed to God's creation. Through these retreats, the youth find refreshment and renewal as they celebrate God's creation.

The retreats are organized by a youth retreat council. These teenagers exercise the freedom to select the spiritual direction of the weekend, the activities, and the focus of the weekend. The weekend nails home a spiritual truth that only a weekend away could really accomplish. With the backdrop of a placid lake and rugged greenery, the teenagers are reminded that God is far greater than their perception of the world.

Have you ever seen the famous poster that depicts a New York City perspective of the world? It shows Park Avenue, the Statue of Liberty, the ocean, and then the rest of the world. Well, this represents the way many urban young people see the world. Their world usually consists of their block, their school, and then the rest of the world. They desire to get out of their environment, but they may need some help to experience that. The urban church has a unique opportunity to expose teenagers to another view of life and the world.

● EVANGELISM INVASIONS—As I mentioned earlier, these outreach events are designed to reach non-Christians through one-on-one sharing and outdoor services. These events occur on the first Saturday of every month. Teenagers invade malls, housing projects, and gang neighborhoods to share the gospel of Christ. These events serve two purposes: to provide opportunities for people to make commitments to Christ and to help the teenagers who share in their community build integrity. They're challenged to actually live the life they're describing to others.

These events create an incredible sense of the power of God. These teenagers actually see the power of God using them to change their friends and neighbors. This is the fleshing out of the Great Commission.

The Power of God

We've seen many lives changed by the power of God. The church stands in the middle of two warring gang factions: the Gangster Disciple Nation and the Black Disciple Nation. These two rival gangs have made their locations clearly known. They have drawn "lines in the sand" to claim their turf. Anyone who enters this turf and chooses to sell drugs or represent the rival gang is certain to face an attack or even death.

This is the story of two young men who grew up on the same block, the best of friends. They attended the same grammar schools, played basketball together, and even had their own dance group. However, the pressure of the gangs was strong. They both decided to join the Black Gangster Disciple Nation. Initially, things went great for both of them. They were cared for by men who seemed to be concerned about their lives and futures. Within the organization, they were taught discipline and business skills.

The boys began as footmen but soon moved up the ranks to become overseers of other young men who would sell and run drugs. Joe and Tom made a vow to honor their gang until the point of death, if necessary. As time progressed, a civil war arose between two factions within the Black Gangster Disciple Nation, and it split in two (Black Disciples and Gangster Disciples). Joe and Tom's friendship also split. A lifetime of laughter, fun, and friendship was severed by gang loyalty. Tom and Joe were now enemies—in the same neighborhood but with different allegiances.

Our church found itself in the middle of these two rival gangs. As a result of this war, I began to communicate with Tom and Joe separately. I would sit on their porches while they drank wine coolers and smoked marijuana, and I noticed that the young men really wanted answers. They hated being in these gangs that seemed to have torn apart the only loving relationships they had known.

They seemed callous and cold during the first visits (the attitude of most urban youth at first contact). I continued to hang out more and more on their porches. Soon they began to predict my coming. The day came when Tom showed up at one of our youth church services. As I preached the gospel and invited young people to make a commitment to Jesus, this young man gave his life to Jesus. Soon after, Joe showed up, and the same thing happened to him.

As they were discipled, these two young men made incredible changes for the Lord. With amazement we watched them come regularly to Bible class, Sunday school, and youth church. Soon Tom was made a junior deacon and Joe became our youth-church drummer.

The gangs weren't pleased with the changes in these young men's lives. Not only had they embarrassed both gangs, but these guys were good money managers. The gangs didn't want to lose their skills. But Joe and Tom knew what they had to do. Both of them approached their leadership and let them know in no uncertain terms that the decisions they had made to commit themselves to Christ were not light ones. They placed their total trust in God's sufficiency.

Normally when young men or women decide to leave a gang, they're violated—either severely beaten or, depending on the rank, even killed. For Tom and Joe, Christian discipleship could literally cost them their lives. After close examination of the church involvement and character change in these two young men, the gangs adopted "hands off" policies for both of them.

Curiosity caused many of the other gang members to marvel at the changes in these two young men's lives and to visit Salem Baptist Church of Chicago. The same living power of God that had changed Tom and Joe transformed the lives of other gang members as well. And the story continues week by week. To God be the glory!

In an area that is plagued with hopelessness, testimonies like this one bring the reality of Christ to the urban setting. In the worship services on Sundays, we allow times of sharing, when other stories are told. Some of the testimonies are as dramatic as the one mentioned above, and others seem more mundane. No matter what, though, after someone shares, it's evident that the living power of God is genuine in the life of this urban youth ministry.

Strengths of This Urban Ministry Model

There's always a danger in developing cookie-cutter ministries. As you read this chapter, my prayer is that you take the "dough" of the concepts and mold them into identifiable pieces that properly fit your ministry. A model is never the actual product. These are merely suggestions, ideas, and comments on years of experience with teenagers in the urban inner city. It's with this understanding that we evaluate the strengths of a ministry like the one described in this chapter.

1. Results

Evangelism, making disciples, and setting people free are the greatest strengths of this model. Since the urban setting is such a hopeless environment, we literally have seen life and hope enter where there had only been death.

2. Need-based ministry

Another great strength of this model is that actual ministry is occurring. As I mentioned earlier in the chapter, ministry means meeting needs. Well, this model of urban youth ministry meets needs in several ways.

● When young people commit their lives to Jesus, they're immediately mentored and discipled in the decision they've made.

● The young people select to minister in the departments that are in line with their gifts and as a result find worth and meaning in being involved in the church. These teenagers actually see their place in proclaiming the Word of God.

● The adults in the congregation have an opportunity to use their gifts as well, in volunteering with the youth ministry in the areas of their strength. Since the youth ministry volunteers are trained and discipled by the youth pastor, they experience great personal growth as well as ministerial expertise.

● The changed lives begin to impact those who aren't Christians. Through church-sponsored outreach events and lifestyle evangelism, many young people are being added to the kingdom and to our local assembly.

3. Church growth

The final strength of this model is that it allows for church growth. As senior pastors attempt to develop and discover new ways to grow their churches, it's interesting to note that specialization is often the answer. Just as in the secular world specializing in a particular area creates growth and greater productivity, the same applies to the church. As the senior pastor releases the care of the young people to another leader, the senior pastor is able to focus on other areas that require immediate attention. With this division of labor, church leadership avoids burnout.

Weaknesses of This Urban Youth Ministry Model

Although we've had tremendous success with this youth ministry model, we've faced some struggles as well.

1. Barriers between adults and teenagers

First of all, we've noticed that with such a strong youth ministry and our own worship service, we have a huge gulf between the adult worship service and the youth worship service. Since the teenagers worship in a separate facility on a weekly basis, some teenagers join our church, participate, and grow without seeing or sometimes even being aware of an adult worship service or our senior pastor. Although we take care every Sunday to place the senior pastor in the prayers of the youth, he is often an abstract figure in a church that is affectionately called the Big Church.

Although this gulf hasn't appeared to be a problem with the adults in the church, it has caused great agony for the youth ministry and its volunteers. When it's time for teenagers to make the transition from youth church to adult church, this transition is often difficult for them. Many have opted to go through the training classes to become youth workers.

We're currently reviewing a possible solution that will allow the high school seniors to interact, worship, and fellowship with the singles classes and other adult programs as a bridge to adult worship.

2. Pride

The second weakness is a false sense of pride among our young people. Healthy confidence and arrogance are quite different. One of the reasons for the immense success of urban street gangs is the need for teenagers to feel that they belong to something. When they find something, they usually decide that thing is the best of all things to belong to. This mentality is present in urban schools, neighborhoods, and other places.

Because these urban teenagers are searching for something significant with which to be associated, many of them believe their ministry is by far better than any other local youth ministry. Where Christ calls for humility and giving all glory to God, many of these teenagers seek to get the glory for ingenious routines, awesome skits, and incredible songs.

3. Need for social empowerment

Not all urban young people fit the stereotypes. They aren't all struggling with gangs, drugs, and unhealthy living. Many of them are in school and have families who are concerned about their futures. There are those, though, who have been incarcerated or on drugs and who don't have high school diplomas or marketable skills. When these young people decide to follow Christ, they often leave the only sources of income, support, and sustenance they've known. Because the developmental needs of these teenagers are so great, it's very difficult for them to get their GEDs, temporary housing, and jobs.

It's difficult to look in the faces of young people who are trying to commit themselves to Christ and his precepts, only to realize the difficulty in finding a viable means of living. This is a great challenge to our youth ministry.

4. Lack of parental involvement

No successful youth ministry can occur apart from the involvement of parents. Because we have such an incredible number of teenagers attending our church and their needs are so varied, it's easy to fail to reach out to the parents.

We conduct quarterly surveys of our teenagers. In these surveys we discover their feelings about Salem Baptist Church of Chicago's youth ministry. We also endeavor to find out about them. We ask them about their modes of transportation to our church. Consistently, 75 to 85 percent of the young people attend our Sunday youth services alone.

We also have discovered that many of their parents aren't Christians. This has proven to be a challenge. When we telephone homes to celebrate the decisions teenagers have made to join our church, the parents sometimes become belligerent about the decisions their children have made without them. In fact, we've found this to be the norm rather than the exception. As a result, we find it difficult to reach the parents of the young people who don't support at home the principles that we're attempting to share. Parent ministry is definitely key, but it's still in the oven of preparation for us.

Putting It Together

Have you ever sat in your living room on Christmas Eve, getting ready to undertake the assembly of an item that looked so simple on the showroom floor? Instead of the seemingly flawless floor model, you're left with a bunch of loose nuts, bolts, bars, and other undefined objects strewn all over the floor. Where do you start?

Well, a message on the box probably gave you certain warnings before you even purchased the item. The message probably told you that assembly would be required for the item to look like it does on the box. In addition, the message probably mentioned the necessity of certain tools to assemble the item. Finally, it probably encouraged you to look at the instructions inside and follow them closely.

Assembly is also required for any urban youth ministry model. As you have read this chapter, my prayer is that the Holy Spirit has shared with you his compassion for the urban teenager. Jesus loves teenagers! But you may have found yourself wondering whether my illustrations and descriptions apply only to my situation. Can this happen in your city? Will the resources be available?

Let me close this chapter by sharing some important assembly requirements. (These will serve as reminders of what we've covered.)

● CUSTOMIZATION—It's important to realize that the model has to be adjusted to your circumstances. "Urban" doesn't always mean inner city. But there are some basic elements in the general structure of any urban youth ministry. Use those ideas that apply to you. On the other hand, the ideas that don't have significance to your setting, place on the shelf for later reference if needed. This book is full of other models that may also apply to your situation.

● A FULL-TIME YOUTH PASTOR—I applaud and celebrate youth leaders, workers, and pastors who can't be full time. Hats off to the laborers who come home from their salaried jobs to load up their cars with teenagers and empty their pockets for chips and sodas for the evening Bible study! You are awesome. Don't be frustrated if you simply don't have enough hours in the day to use the creative gifts God has given you. Do what you can with the resources God has provided. Use what you can from this chapter.

● VOLUNTEERS—Youth ministry volunteers are the bolts that tie the ministry together. In order to achieve the breadth of ministry outlined in this chapter, you must have a crew of committed people who are dedicated to meeting the needs of teenagers. No matter what the creative gifts of the leader, he or she will be able to reach only as far as the arms of the staff. The volunteers give more eyes, ears, hands, and hearts to care for the group.

You can recruit volunteers through your church bulletin or even through comments and emphasis from your senior pastor. You can even observe adults who seem to enjoy hanging around teenagers and ask for their support on a project. Watch the cream rise to the top!

● PRAYER—Prayer brings in the teenagers. Prayer touches the hearts of adults within the congregation to work with youth. Prayer is depending on God more than fancy fliers and catchy slogans to bring in the results. As you finish this chapter, I challenge you to enter into a genuine time of prayer (two-way communication) with the Lord. It's in these quiet moments in God's presence that ideas, answers, and people are raised up for ministry.

● THE BIBLE—The Word of God is the instruction manual for this model. If we want to know how to put something together, we always seek the manufacturer. Since God is the author of all things, we should consult God's Word about the development of a model for urban youth ministry. God's Word holds examples of every form of ministry to teenagers we can imagine. The assumption is that any church that adopts a model like the one outlined in this chapter will hold to the Bible as the manual for every activity, every outing, and every meeting. When each department and activity is built on Scripture, the chances of the ministry folding or failing are next to nothing.

● YOUR SENIOR PASTOR'S SUPPORT—The senior pastor is another factor that can cause this model to soar or sink. If for some reason the senior pastor doesn't desire to support the youth ministry with finances, encouragement, or even acknowledgment from the pulpit, your response should be prayer and submission to the pastor's authority. When we attempt to carry out our own agendas and our own plans, we have completely missed God's purpose for the church—to be one body.

Many of the successes I've had have been the result of a senior pastor who has supported the youth ministry at every turn. But if your situation isn't like that, don't you go ahead of your leader. Allow God to do the work.

● EXCITEMENT—You as the youth leader must be excited. One reason for the success of youth ministry at Salem Baptist Church of Chicago is the energy level of its leaders. Teenagers are full of energy. It's crucial that we as leaders show some excitement and life as we share with them biblical truths.

● A TEACHABLE SPIRIT—To be successful in urban ministry, the youth leader must be willing to learn new ways and methods. Since you're reading this book, it's obvious that you want to learn all you can about youth ministry. I applaud you for this.

● VISION—When you're sitting in your living room on Christmas Eve trying to put together that complex item, it helps to have a picture in your mind of what the finished item should look like. This vision will drive you to complete the assembly and to do it right. When the item isn't looking like the vision you have, although the process might take some time, you continue to work.

A youth leader or worker who has a vision of what the Lord has called the church's youth ministry program to become will also be driven by that vision. If that picture in your mind is based on the Word of God in your heart, nothing can deter you from seeing that picture become reality.

As this chapter concludes, I'm reminded of a youth worker from another church who came to visit our ministry. With a look of awe, this young lady stated that what she was seeing was a miracle. She found it hard to believe that such a ministry could exist in the heart of Chicago's inner city.

I looked at this woman and told her that God had been gracious, but what she was seeing was no miracle! With an almost frightened look, this youth worker must have thought I was refusing to give glory to God for what he had done at Salem Baptist Church of Chicago. This was far from the truth.

I walked to the water cooler outside my office, filled a glass with water, brought it back, and placed it on the desk. I began to gaze at the glass and express awe that it was full. I asked her whether the full glass of water was miraculous or not. Somewhat annoyed, she responded dryly that it wasn't miraculous.

I explained that God had made the glass, the water, and the ability for me to connect the two together. But the effort I had expended in pouring the water into the glass was what had made the glass full. I reminded her of the youth ministry. The success of the ministry is the result of leaders and volunteers pouring themselves into the lives of teenagers.

When you see teenagers in love with God and God's Word, you're not seeing some incredible phenomenon that miraculously happened without the efforts of people. God graciously gave us the young people and the volunteers. He supplied us with the desire and energy to reach a lost generation for Christ. And we simply poured into them that which was poured into us.

As you go forward in urban ministry, don't gape in awe at what others have done. Get ready for what the Lord is getting ready to do through you. At the end of your day, you'll look and thank God for all of his gifts that have enabled you and your team to point urban teenagers to Christ.

CHAPTER 3:
Reconstructing Family Life

Family-Based Youth Ministry

CHAP CLARK, Ph.D.
Associate Professor of Youth and Family Ministries at Fuller Theological Seminary in Pasadena, California

and PAMELA J. ERWIN
Coordinator of Youth and Family Ministries and Adjunct Professor at Denver Seminary in Denver, Colorado

Tom and Cathy are the parents of Caitlyn, a junior in high school. Tom and Cathy don't attend church, but Caitlyn occasionally attends youth group at a nearby church with one of her friends from school. For the past couple of months, Tom and Cathy have begun to suspect that Caitlyn is using drugs. All the typical signs are present: She's always been a good student, but now she's struggling to keep her grades up and often misses classes because she "doesn't feel well." Caitlyn has withdrawn from many of her former friends—she's found a new group of friends that make Tom and Cathy nervous. Her parents have no idea where to turn for help.

Todd, the youth worker at the local church, is concerned too. Caitlyn still comes to church occasionally, but Todd knows something is different. The friend she comes with is concerned about Caitlyn's new friends and the drug use she's almost certain of. She's expressed her concerns to Todd.

Todd briefly thought about contacting Caitlyn's parents, but he had never met them. He was afraid they might resent his interfering, so he never called. Now Todd and Caitlyn's parents are watching in anguish as Caitlyn becomes more and more lost to them.

The parents are struggling alone. The youth worker is struggling alone. Everyone is concerned about Caitlyn, but everyone feels helpless to do anything about the situation.

By partnering with Caitlyn's parents, Todd could act as a resource for the parents in a couple of ways. First, he could empower the parents to handle their parental responsibilities by offering support and encouragement. Second, he could provide practical training in skills and education, and if necessary, he could refer the parents to appropriate professional sources of help.

An Extended Church Community

Allison is a freshman at her local community college. As a child, she went to church every Sunday with her family. As a young teenager, she became active in her church youth group. She enjoyed hanging out with other teenagers and her youth leaders. They could always count on Allison to be at the youth group Bible studies, retreats, and mission trips. After Allison graduated from high school, she didn't feel she was a part of the youth group anymore. More and more, she slept in on Sunday mornings. By the time she started college in the fall, Allison no longer attended church. She didn't feel as if she fit in anywhere. What had happened? During her middle school and high school years her sole focus had been the youth group. She now felt no connection to her church outside the youth group.

According to Mark DeVries, "Apart from the family...the church may be the only lifelong nurturing structure left."[1] Young people are more likely to maintain a growing, sustained faith if youth workers partner with the extended church community rather than separating young people from the rest of the church. We can, through this partnership, lay the foundation for faith and relationships with Jesus that will carry young people through all the stages of their lives.

Today's young people are growing up in a world where drug use is rampant among teenagers and adults; a world wracked by violence; a world that glorifies athletic prowess and beautiful bodies, not heroes. The evidence of the influence of our culture on young people is overwhelming. Drug use among eighth graders more than doubled between 1991 and 1996.[2] Teenagers in the United States are twelve times more likely to be killed by guns than in any other industrialized country.[3] Between 1986 and 1993, the number of abused or neglected children increased 98 percent.[4] It takes a community effort to bring life in the midst of this chaos. To touch young peoples' lives, youth workers must join forces with parents and families.

In this chapter we present a model of family-based youth ministry that involves partnering with essentially two families: the nuclear family and the extended church family. This approach basically restores two crucial elements currently missing from many teenagers' lives. We propose a shift in the traditional thinking of how we do youth ministry. Since young people don't exist in a vacuum, youth ministry can't be planned as if young people function independently of families or the rest of the local church.

This model of youth ministry involves the family, the youth ministry, and the extended church community pulling together to surround each young person with a healthy, nurturing environment. Functioning as a team, adults join forces in reconstructing a vibrant family and community life to care for adolescents.

How Traditional Youth Ministry Hurts Families

As youth workers, we spend much of our time planning youth events and making quick decisions. Sometimes in the midst of these responsibilities, we unintentionally hurt or weaken the families of the young people we work with. We offer this section not as an attack on youth workers, but to suggest that we function together *with* parents in reaching out to teenagers. Here are eight mistakes we often make that hurt families.

1. Not considering family times and needs when scheduling youth events

Just recently, a mom of a teenager called to discuss her concerns about the calendar of events she had received from her church youth pastor. She wanted to know if she was being overly sensitive to the fact that at least four nights of meetings and activities were scheduled every week for her tenth-grade son, plus regular weekend activities. In addition, her son was on the high school football team. "I feel like I'm competing with the church to spend time with my son. The only time I get to see him is for about fifteen seconds as he collapses through the door most nights, heading for his room to finish his homework. I wish the youth pastor would consider families as important as youth group activities."

Not only do our full schedules take young people away from their families, the many activities often add to their stress. School counselors and therapists know that stress is one of the most crucial issues in the lives of most young people. Teenagers are pulled in many different directions and face a variety of expectations. It may be time to evaluate the importance and frequency of the meetings and activities in your youth ministry program. Remember the adage "Less is more."

2. Assuming the role of parents

Joe loves volunteering with his church's youth group. He has grown especially close to Brian, one of the students. Brian and Joe spend most of their free time together playing basketball, working together on Brian's homework and school projects, and talking about Brian's current problems and future plans. Occasionally, Joe has noticed Brian's dad giving him strange looks as Brian sits with Joe during Sunday morning worship. "Maybe he's jealous," Joe says to himself. It never occurs to Joe to talk to Brian's dad or to encourage Brian in his relationship with his father.

Without a doubt, we need to develop strong relationships with the young people in our ministries. We all want volunteers who are willing to become actively involved with young people. Young people need as many significant relationships with adult Christians as possible. But those relationships must foster and encourage young people's relationships with their parents.

3. Making parents look bad

Karen was serving in her first youth ministry position, leading a small group. She was anxious to be accepted by the senior high girls. Meetings with her small group often became gripe sessions about the girls' parents. In an effort to be considered "one of the girls," she often joined in criticizing the parents, sharing her own horror stories from her teenage years. One morning after a small-group meeting, Karen was surprised to find an angry mom in her office, demanding to know why she constantly made her feel like an incompetent parent. By joining in with her daughter, Karen had given the impression that she considered this mom a bad parent.

In an attempt to gain the acceptance of young people, we often denigrate parents. We must be balanced when listening to young people regarding their conflicts with parents—remember, you're hearing only one side of the story. We can listen without joining in or making value judgments on the parents.

4. Not keeping parents informed

Jim and Sally had planned a family vacation for the second week of July. They were looking forward to getting away and spending some quality time camping with their three children. Two weeks before their vacation, Chad, their fourteen-year-old, came home from youth group all excited. Handing his mom a flier, Chad said, "Jake has planned a trail ride for all the new ninth-grade guys. I can't wait. Is it all right if I go?" As Sally began reading the flier, her heart sank. The trip was scheduled for July, right in the middle of their family vacation time. Now she and Jim faced a dilemma: demand that Chad attend the family vacation or allow him to go on the trail ride and miss the family vacation. Neither option was appealing.

Last-minute planning often forces parents to make difficult choices. While it's impossible to avoid every scheduling conflict, giving parents reasonable notification of upcoming events allows parents to rearrange their plans and to incorporate youth events into their schedules.

5. Not encouraging or offering support for families

Molly and John had been married for ten years. They each had two children from a previous marriage, and they constantly were juggling the demands of visitation schedules and blending two families. Two of their children, Josh and Jacob, were active in their church's youth group. Betsy, the youth pastor, was well aware of Molly and John's situation, but the adults in the youth ministry seldom had any contact with Molly or John. The only time Betsy had talked with John was when Jacob had gotten in trouble on a weekend retreat.

Many of the families of the teenagers in our youth groups are facing huge pressures—single parenthood, divorce, blended families, and others. There are several ways we can offer support and encouragement to parents. For many parents, simply knowing us and knowing that we're there if they need encouragement may be enough to help relieve some of their stress.

6. Undermining parents' judgment or authority

Aaron often had lunch with students at the local high school. Occasionally he would take a few of the students to a nearby burger joint. When he picked up a group of four tenth-grade guys one Friday, Jerrod, one of the boys, told Aaron that his mom didn't want him to go off campus for lunch. "Oh, it's OK. I'm sure your mom won't mind if you go with me. Come on, let's go." Aaron never stopped to think of the long-term effects of encouraging Jerrod to disobey his parents.

Sometimes it's as simple as stopping to think about the consequences of what we say or do in front of kids. They hear plenty of messages encouraging them to ignore or disrespect their parents; we should always encourage them to honor and obey their parents.

7. Not including families in youth events

Yolanda is an extremely organized youth worker. She's great at planning ahead for social activities, Bible studies, and retreats. As usual she sent out parent calendars in August so parents could plan for the upcoming year. A few days after the calendars went out, she received a call from Pete, the father of Luke, one of the middle school boys. "I just got this year's youth calendar. It looks great!. I was wondering, though, if you've ever thought about a father-son rafting trip. Luke and I were talking, and we'd love to do something like that with other dads and their sons." Yolanda had always assumed that teenagers didn't want to spend time with their parents and that parents wanted the break from their kids.

An occasional family outing or parent-teenager night will foster a sense of unity between parents and the youth group, in addition to providing quality time for parents and teenagers to interact.

8. Failing to connect teenagers with the extended church family

Doug recently got a promotion with his company and moved from Connecticut to California. A single father with two teenagers, Doug immediately became involved with a singles group in a nearby church; while his sons, Jack and Jeremy, joined the youth group. Doug had bought a great house in a wonderful neighborhood with a good school system, but his work schedule and the demands of single-parenthood prevented him from building many relationships in his community. They had been in California four months when the holiday season rolled around. Doug's singles group scheduled lots of activities, but none of them included children. Jack and Jeremy were becoming an integral part of the youth group, but they had few connections with adults. Far away from extended family, Doug, Jack, and Jeremy felt increasingly isolated and alone.

For a variety of reasons, many families have lost their close connections to extended family and to communities. The youth group is a natural place to connect teenagers and their parents with the larger church to help restore community and a sense of family.

Partnering With Families and the Extended Church Community

So what does a model of cooperative youth and family ministry look like? There are a variety of models that work in various situations. When putting a model in place, a youth worker must consider a number of factors: the size of the church and the youth program, the philosophy of the church, the demographics of the church and the community, and others. What we're suggesting is a general philosophy of youth ministry that unites families and youth workers within the context of the larger church community. The result is a three-way partnership between a youth ministry program, families, and the local church as a whole. The following diagram reflects this philosophy.

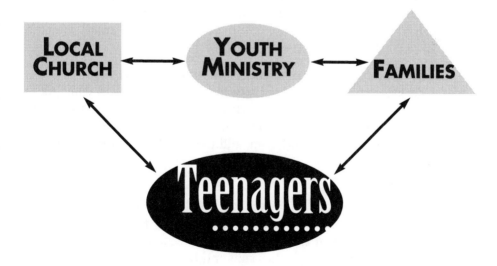

There are three overriding qualities in any family-based youth ministry program: It serves to strengthen families, to connect youth ministry to the extended church, and to help the church function as a community of believers.

STRENGTHENS FAMILIES

Encouraging and supporting parents through education and training helps them develop competency and belief in their capabilities as parents. This in itself is beneficial.

In addition, though, scheduling family-wide events will serve to connect parents with other parents. Besides providing needed adult relationships, this type of community often reminds parents that they aren't alone—that others are going through similar experiences—and gives parents opportunities to benefit from the wisdom of parents who have weathered similar situations. In a sense the youth ministry and the church serve as coaches, providing resources and encouragement for parents to effectively do their job.

CONNECTS THE YOUTH MINISTRY TO THE EXTENDED CHURCH

When the church and the youth ministry come together in a unified effort to reach teenagers and their families, two things happen. First, teenagers will be connected to the rest of the church. For example, instead of planning a youth-parent picnic or fellowship, plan a churchwide family fellowship. Teenagers will then have the opportunity to get to know single adults, younger children, and senior adults. These kinds of relationships are vital to a young person's well-being.

Second, this kind of ministry will very often draw parents into the overall ministry of the church. Many of the families of teenagers are unchurched. Through a team effort, you can provide entry points for parents to become a part of your fellowship.

HELPS THE CHURCH FUNCTION AS A COMMUNITY OF BELIEVERS

In this model of youth ministry, the church becomes a vital link for families and teenagers—a place where the family can be nurtured and cared for. The church community joins with the family to celebrate and worship, to encourage and train, and to disciple and support them.

Guidelines

Family-based youth ministry can be adapted to reflect the particular dynamics of local churches and their ministries. Here are a few guidelines for implementing this type of program.

● Get the support of other staff and the church leadership.

● Be willing to let go of programs or events, if needed, in order to partner with other ministries in the church.

● Identify, with the help of other church leaders, your areas of responsibilities. For example, if you decide to host churchwide or intergenerational events, decide who will be responsible for planning them.

● Begin to implement changes gradually, perhaps over a one- to two-year period.

Making Changes

This kind of ministry requires a shift in thinking—to an attitude that the youth worker, the church, and the family are part of a team seeking to impact the lives of adolescents. As youth leaders plan, we suggest asking the following two questions: *How can I be of help to parents?* and *How can the extended church community be involved in ministry to young people?*

The following ideas may help to usher in a shift in thinking as you begin to do cooperative youth and family ministry.

● Meet with other pastoral staff to brainstorm how you can be more effective in helping parents. Normally youth programs are planned separately and independently from the other programs of the church. Meet with other pastoral staff to look at ways you can improve or eliminate programs to maximize the benefit to families.

● Work with your church leadership to decide what areas your ministry will focus on: nurturing and counseling families, building community, or training and equipping parents. You may want to do all three, depending on the needs of your church.

● Talk to leaders of other programs such as children's ministries, Sunday school, and women's ministries to solicit their input and suggestions for how your ministry could be more "family friendly."

● Bring in family experts such as substance abuse counselors, school counselors, and family therapists to talk about specific issues with your leadership team. Do this two or three times a year, and cover a variety of subjects such as family stress; and children of blended, divorced, and single-parent families. The more you and your other leaders understand families, the more effective your ministry to them will be.

● Take time to discuss with parents their views of how the church can best minister to families.

Implementing a Family-Based Approach to Youth Ministry

This section offers ten suggestions for implementing a family-based youth ministry program.

1. Develop strong relationships with a few parents.

At their annual planning retreat, Janice's ministry team identifies key parents for each adult youth worker to get to know during the next year. Each leader commits to building relationships with three or four parents. In the four years they've been intentionally seeking to develop relationships with parents, their youth program has been greatly enriched through the support and encouragement of the parents. And the parents are more receptive and eager to hear from the youth workers when issues or concerns do come up.

Listening to parents and encouraging them in their role fosters ministry as a cooperative effort. The stronger your relationships with parents, the better you'll know each other's needs. Parents will be more likely to encourage and support you in your ministry, but more important, you'll build relationships that will allow you to minister better to teenagers.

Here are some ways to nurture relationships with parents.

● Make a five- to ten-minute phone call to one parent each week.

● Have a breakfast or lunch meeting with two parents each quarter.

● Make it a point to ask a couple of parents each month as you meet up with them in church, "What can we be doing for you?"

● At every game or other school event you attend, be sure to talk to at least one parent about how that person's daughter or son is doing.

● Once a quarter, host a prayer time for parents. Find out what the burning issues are for parents, and pray with them for their children.

● Once a year, ask parents to fill out a questionnaire, identifying the top needs of their families. (See the sample questionnaire on pages 57-58.) Provide a copy of the results for your senior pastor.

Parent Questionnaire

Name: _____

Name(s) of child(ren) in youth program:

_____

Marital status: ___ Married to first spouse   ___ Never married
                  ___ Divorced   ___ Divorced and remarried
                  ___ Separated   ___ Widowed
                  ___ Widowed and remarried

Spouse's name (if applicable): _____

Other parental figures in your child(ren)'s life (stepparents, grandparents, etc.):

_____

Siblings (names and ages): _____

_____

Occupations of parents:
Mother: _____   Father: _____
Stepfather: _____   Stepmother: _____

Please identify the five top concerns for your children:

___ alcohol and drugs   ___ school work/homework
___ communication   ___ relationships with other family
___ discipline   members
___ faith in Christ   ___ self-esteem
___ friends   ___ sexuality
___ gangs   ___ stress
___ knowledge of Scriptures   ___ TV/movies/music
___ loneliness/isolation   ___ violence
___ other _____

Please identify the top five concerns for your marriage and/or family:

___ blended family issues   ___ sex
___ careers   ___ spiritual growth
___ communication   ___ stress
___ conflict resolution   ___ substance abuse
___ extended family issues   ___ time as a couple
___ finances   ___ time as a family

___ fulfillment   ___ trust
___ intimacy   ___ other:_____

How can the church pray for or minister to you and your family?

_____

_____

_____

Do the days and times of our youth programming work for you? _____ If no,
what times would work best? _____

_____

What do you appreciate most about our church? _____

_____

_____

_____

Other comments: _____

_____

_____

_____

_____

_____

_____

_____

_____

_____

_____

_____

_____

_____

_____

_____

_____

_____

_____

_____

2. Communicate, communicate, communicate.

Many of the conflicts and misunderstandings we encounter could be avoided if we communicated effectively with parents. There are a variety of ways you can keep parents informed and involved in the youth ministry.

● Prepare a parent newsletter once a quarter. Include information on upcoming events and activities. Be sure to list pertinent details parents will need to know such as costs, registration dates, emergency phone numbers, and locations. Also include sections on parenting helps, current youth culture, and other helpful information for parents. If your budget allows, mail the newsletters to parents instead of handing them out to teenagers to bring home. (You may want to enlist a parent to put the newsletter together. This may even be a good opportunity for the parent to work with his or her teenager or another teenager who is interested in desktop publishing.)

● Set up a "parents table" near your youth area or possibly in an area where adults from the extended church community will have access to it. (This is a good way to spark the interest of singles and other adults and encourage them to be involved with young people.) Provide current issues of parenting magazines such as Living With Teenagers, ParentLife, Single Parent Family, and Urban Family, new books and videos on parenting and current issues, resources for parents on youth issues (drug abuse, gangs, school struggles).

● Send home fliers regarding special events such as retreats, mission trips, and conferences at least eight weeks ahead of time.

● At the beginning of each school year, provide parents with a youth ministry calendar showing regular meetings and activities as well as special events for the upcoming year. It's best to actually plan these events a year in advance, if possible. The further ahead you can plan, the better for parents.

3. Be sensitive to family time and commitments.

Today's young people and their families face stress like never before. Part of that stress is directly related to the busyness of their lives. Without thinking, we often add to that stress with the number of meetings and activities we schedule and the impression we give that young people must attend everything we program. Here are some suggestions to help create sensitivity in your programming.

● First evaluate your own schedule. If your schedule is packed and leaves little time for personal commitments and spiritual growth, most likely you have too many meetings and activities for young people. Begin by looking at how busy you are and canceling anything that reasonably can be eliminated.

● Make sure to have copies of school calendars (and community calendars, if available) when scheduling. Be sensitive to times when parents normally schedule vacation times. Notice when school and community calendars are full, and schedule as few events during that time as possible. (If possible, it's a good idea to develop relationships with school leaders. Work together with them in planning schedules.)

● Evaluate meeting times. See if some can be combined with other meetings or eliminated entirely.

● Give students freedom to miss meetings and events when they conflict with family times.

4. Be a resource for families.

As you develop relationships with parents, you'll begin to identify the leading issues for parents in your community. Knowing what these needs are will enable you to be a good resource for parents and families. Here are some ways you can address those needs.

● Every couple of months or once a quarter, bring in an expert on a particular issue. Be creative in finding people to speak to parents. You may have community leaders in your church who have expertise in areas such as drug use, violence, teenage pregnancy, and stress. Local social service organizations or school officials are often willing to come and speak to parents. Encourage young people to attend with their families when appropriate.

● Create a mini-library (or a large one if you have the funding). You can set up something as simple as a table in your office where parents can check out books on adolescent and parenting issues. Don't forget that parents are growing too; offer some books on spiritual growth and development. If your budget allows, offer one or two videos on parenting issues as well.

● Maintain a current contact list for parents. Include crisis hot line numbers. Also include a list of counselors who specialize in adolescent and family issues, residential and day-treatment facilities, and school counselors.

● Maintain a list of books and videos that parents might find helpful. (A parent or another adult might volunteer to maintain this list.)

● Occasionally offer parenting workshops. If appropriate, encourage teenagers and adults from the larger church community to attend.

5. Let parents know when they're doing a good job.

If you ask parents to tell you where they fail as parents, most parents will easily answer. If you ask them to name ways they're good parents, most will have to think hard before answering. You can help parents feel good about being parents, and help them be better parents, by helping them identify ways they're good parents. Here are a few simple ways to encourage parents.

● Call two or three parents a week and tell them good things about their children.

● Drop parents notes occasionally to let them know how much you appreciate their children.

● When you see parents at church or at the mall, praise them for the good job they're doing. (Be sincere.)

6. Include parents in youth events.

Schedule occasional events that include parents and families. Family events will give young people time with their parents, allow you to get to know parents better, and provide opportunities for parents to get to know each other better. You can bring parents and teenagers together by planning

● family camping trips,

● parent-teenager rafting trips,

● family mission trips,

● service projects that include families, and

● father/son, father/daughter, mother/daughter, mother/son events. (Be sure to provide substitute parents for young people who need them.)

7. Plan intergenerational churchwide events.

You can encourage cross-generational relationships by welcoming adults of all ages as volunteer leaders and by planning a few intergenerational events each year. A few ideas include

● a churchwide picnic hosted by young people;

● a luncheon or breakfast for teenagers hosted by senior adults or lunch or breakfast for seniors hosted by teenagers; and

● "big buddy" events (picnics, parents' night out, Sunday school classes) with teenagers hosting preschool or elementary-age children.

8. Recruit volunteers from throughout the extended church community.

Young people relate to all different types of people. Some are attracted to middle-aged, quiet, introverted computer geniuses; some relate to the skater college students, and others (especially younger adolescents) relate to older adults. Don't be surprised at the diversity of the adolescents you work with. Remember that diversity in enlisting volunteers. Be intentional about asking a variety of personality types and ages to work with your youth group.

9. Develop mentoring relationships with teenagers.

It's vital that we provide as many opportunities as possible for young people to have close, one-on-one or small-group relationships with adults. The contact can be minimal or in-depth. The important factor is to have teenagers in relationships with a number of adults. Here are a few ways to accomplish that.

● Organize small-group Bible studies of five to eight students led by an adult or a couple. (Young people also need to see positive marriage relationships modeled.)

● Enlist a group of adults to telephone two to three teenagers a week to ask them how they're doing. Young people may seem initially hesitant, but eventually they'll look forward to the contact, knowing that someone is taking a personal interest in them. (Seniors are usually willing to do this kind of ministry when they may be hesitant to be regular volunteers with the youth program.)

● Enlist adults to be one-on-one mentors, willing to meet with young people on a weekly or biweekly basis. If possible suggest a six-month to one-year commitment. It would be helpful to offer training for adults willing to invest themselves in this type of ministry. (For more information, see chapter 4 of this book.)

● Enlist adults to host young people with them at their jobs for a day of job watching. This could be set up all for one particular day, or you could work with individual adults to schedule one or two days a year.

10. Work with the extended church community to include teenagers.

One of the goals of a cooperative youth and family ministry is to encourage young people toward long-term faith and a connection to the church that lasts beyond high school or college. We can assist this process by providing opportunities for young people to be actively involved in various areas of church life.

● WORSHIP AND PRAISE—Students who are gifted musically can be part of the music and worship ministry of the church in the worship team, band, orchestra, or choir.

● DRAMA—If your church has a drama team, teenagers who are interested could be given the opportunity to be a part of the team.

● RITES OF PASSAGE—Develop a system that enables teenagers to have greater responsibility in church leadership as they mature. For example, sixth and seventh graders might help usher, pass out bulletins, and greet guests; twelfth graders might help teach Sunday school to younger children.

● LORD'S SUPPER—In one local urban church, the young people are responsible for preparing the elements and distributing them to the congregation, with adult supervision.

● BAPTISM—This same urban church, which practices adult baptism, encourages teenagers to baptize other teenagers they have discipled or have led into a relationship with Jesus Christ. This can be very significant for both teenagers.

Closing Thoughts

The most important factor in establishing a family-based youth ministry is a shift in thinking. Once you begin to consider your ministry as part of a team effort of parents, youth workers, and the church community at large, you'll then be able to identify ways your ministry might be harmful to families and then adjust your planning and programming to be more family friendly. Instituting huge programs of family ministry, while good, may not be necessary. The changes may be subtle but rewarding.

Begin with a few steps: Develop relationships with parents, knock out a few unnecessary meetings and events, and add a family event here and there. You'll be surprised at how family friendly your program will become.

(For more information on how to your church can become family friendly, see *The Family-Friendly Church* by Ben Freudenburg with Rick Lawrence, published by Group Publishing, Inc.)

ENDNOTES

1. Mark DeVries, *Family-Based Youth Ministry* (Downers Grove, IL: InterVarsity Press, 1994), 116.

2. "Same Story, Different Year," Youthworker Update (February 1997), 3.

3. "Dying by Gunfire," Youthworker Update (March 1997), 4.

4. "Child Abuse on the Rise," Youthworker Update (November 1996), 1.

CHAPTER 4:
Intentional Connections

Using Mentoring in Youth Ministry

WAYNE RICE

Co-Founder of Youth Specialties and Director of Understanding Your Teenager in Lakeside, California

Every Saturday morning at five, Tom Jenkins loads two surfboards into the back of his Ford Explorer and makes the short drive to La Jolla where some of the best waves in Southern California wait to be conquered. On the way, he stops to pick up his young friend Chris, a high school sophomore. Chris doesn't have the experience Tom has accumulated over some twenty-five years of surfing, but he's getting better with every outing. Afterward they stop for a Mexican breakfast at Roberto's taco shop and talk about the waves, the week, and their walk with Jesus Christ. Chris, who lives with his mother and his two sisters, has learned from Tom not only how to surf, but also what it means to be a man of God.

• • • • • • • •

Doris VanderStelt has been living alone since her husband passed away four years ago. The sixty-two-year-old grandmother occupies much of her time painting watercolor landscapes of farms, barns, and old houses scattered around the Michigan countryside. Doris also spends quite a lot of time with Abbie, a fifteen-year-old girl who Doris "adopted" two years ago through her church's Adopt-a-Teenager program. At first, all Doris did was pray for Abbie and send her little notes of encouragement. But lately Abbie has been coming to visit Doris almost every day. Since her mom and dad broke up two months ago, Abbie has needed someone to talk to—and she has found that someone in Doris. Doris, on the other hand, has found in Abbie not only a friend, but an *opportunity to make a difference in someone's life.*

• • • • • • • •

It's Confirmation Sunday, that special day when–after completing several months of study and preparation–a group of young people stands nervously before the congregation to answer questions, recite their vows, and share their testimonies. This is followed by a charge from the pastor who confers upon them the rights and privileges of church membership. Among those standing at the front of the church this year is Jim Buckaloo, a thirty-seven-year-old drywall contractor. He can hardly hold back the tears as he listens to his fifteen-year-old friend Kevin boldly proclaim his faith with the congregation. Jim is standing next to Kevin because six months ago Jim signed on to be a confirmation mentor. Since that time he and Kevin have spent a lot of time together–studying Scripture, learning lessons, participating in the required activities, and preparing for today's ceremony. What Jim feels now as he listens to Kevin is not only pride and joy–but the satisfaction of knowing that both of their lives have been deeply enriched by their shared experience.

• • • • • • • •

Tom Jenkins, Doris VanderStelt, and Jim Buckaloo are very special people. Unlike the vast majority of adults who avoid contact with teenagers, each of them has chosen to be a friend to at least one. Tom, Doris, and Jim aren't professional youth workers, counselors, or teachers, but ordinary adults who have volunteered to make a difference in the lives of kids. They represent a growing positive trend in youth ministry. They are *mentors*.

What Is Mentoring?

In Homer's *Odyssey*, the Greek warrior Odysseus leaves his wife and his young son, Telemachus, at home while he journeys to fight in the Trojan War. To ensure that his son is adequately cared for, Odysseus appoints a teacher named Mentor to tutor the boy and to act as a guardian and friend while he is away. The siege of Troy lasts ten years, and it takes Odysseus another ten years to find his way home. When he finally does return, he finds that Telemachus has developed into a fine young man, thanks to the faithful tutelage of Mentor.[1]

This three-thousand-year-old story—which gives us the modern term "mentor" to describe a close, trusted, experienced counselor and guide—reminds us of a lot of single-parent homes today. Telemachus, like so many of today's kids, grew up in a home without a father. But he did have Mentor, an adult companion who cared about him and taught him what he needed to know.

Every young person—whether in a single-parent home or not—needs a Mentor. While most modern parents aren't leaving home to fight wars, they find it no less difficult today to provide for their children all they need to become healthy, self-reliant adults. Even in families where both mother and father are present, young adolescents still look outside the home for affirmation and guidance. Unfortunately for many kids, all they find are peers, pop culture, and the exploitation of the media.

The International Youth Foundation puts it this way: "Every young person needs at least one adult who is irrationally committed to their well-being. Millions of children grow up virtually alone—disconnected from adults. No love. No supervision. No positive role models. Yet these young people must still find their way—they still grow up to become adults. Children can endure the most miserable conditions—even thrive in the midst of them—if they have at least one loving adult committed to their success."[2]

That's what mentoring is all about. Mentoring happens when adults commit themselves to young people, not because they have to, but because they *want* to. Urie Bronfenbrenner of Cornell University describes this as having an "irrational emotional attachment" to a young person. What makes it irrational is that it communicates to the young person that he or she is special, wonderful, and precious, even though there may be significant evidence to the contrary. It is, in Bronfenbrenner's words, "the illusion that comes with love."[3]

A Last Line of Defense

Among the many reasons mentoring is important, perhaps no reason is more compelling than the fact that *mentors are the last line of defense against the negative influences of peer pressure and the media.*

I often ask people this question: Who or what is the most powerful influence on today's teenagers? The popular consensus seems pretty much unanimous. It's the peer group. How else do we explain the fact that so many kids look alike, talk alike, and act alike? Teenagers do what the crowd does. If anybody has a flock mentality, it's teenagers.

But before we jump to conclusions, let's keep in mind first of all that every age group tends to look alike, talk alike, and act alike. Check out a retirement community sometime and see how many seniors are wearing baggy shorts and backward ball caps. Not too many.

But what about *significant* influence—the kind that shapes values and determines the kind of person someone will become? Who or what is the most powerful influence on teenagers when it comes to *ultimate* issues? Numerous studies have been done to find the answer to this question, and consistently researchers say that the top five influencers of teenagers are, in order (1) parents, (2) the extended family, (3) adults outside the home, (4) peers, (5) the community, and (6) the media.[4]

Such research often seems contradicted by today's youth culture. It doesn't take a rocket scientist to see that teenagers today are overwhelmed by peer pressure and the negative influences of the media. How do we explain studies that downplay such enormous influences?

Here's one explanation. Researchers generally get their data by asking people questions. For example, teenagers are asked, "Who or what is the most important influence in your life?" Or adults are asked, "Who or what influenced you the most when you were a teenager?" Questions like these often produce answers that are often more wishful thinking than reality. In other words, when teenagers say they look to parents, to grandparents, or to adults outside the home for influence, they may be expressing what they *wish* were true more than what is *actually* true.

But the results are revealing, nevertheless. What these studies tell us is that teenagers do look first to significant adults in their lives for influence. They look to their parents, then to other family members, then to other adults who are "irrationally committed" to them. As author H. Stephen Glenn once put it, "Historically, when kids start to individuate from their parents, what they needed most were grandmas, grandpas, aunts, uncles, long-term family friends, to bond with and to mentor them. Those are gone for most kids today."[5]

Who influenced you when you were a teenager? When I reflect on my adolescence, I'm convinced that I stayed out of serious trouble because I had too many people to disappoint. I had parents, grandparents, uncles, aunts, cousins, teachers, coaches, and lots of people at church—who cared about me. They had a tremendous influence on my life.

Unfortunately many kids today have none of the above. Parents are absent, the extended family is dead, and few kids have even one adult outside the home who cares about them. As a result, the peer group and the media have become the dominant influences on their lives.

The peer group exerts a powerful influence on millions of kids today, but it's only influence by default. It's influence given to it by a culture that has abandoned its young. But when parents are there for their kids—and when young people are surrounded by adults who truly care about them—the peer group is virtually de-fanged. It and the media are stripped of their power over kids. That's why it's so important for youth workers to take the lead in equipping the entire church to become the extended family of God that it was meant to be. Kids really do want guidance and direction from people who are older and wiser than they are. This is the rationale, the reason, for developing a mentoring program.

Mentoring as Youth Ministry

Youth ministry has always included mentoring. Every youth worker knows the best kind of youth ministry is centered not on programs, but on relationships.

But youth workers also know that it's very difficult, if not impossible, to develop meaningful relationships with more than just a few kids. And even if it *were* possible, there are always a few kids who need someone else—someone who is able to relate to them better because of age, sex, personality, interests, or other characteristics. No one person is able to relate well to everybody.

Sometimes we try to overcome this problem by recruiting a few volunteer youth workers who can help share the youth ministry load. We get them involved in the youth ministry program as chaperones, counselors, small-group leaders, and the like, and we also ask them to "get to know a few kids." But often we encounter resistance from adults who are already too busy or who believe they're being asked to do "what the church is paying you to do." Those who do volunteer are often worked so hard that they become frustrated, exhausted, or both and end up quitting.

That's why we need a new understanding of youth ministry in the church. It's no longer acceptable to think of it as something that can be done by one person—a "hired gun"—or even a small group of people. The church is the family of God, and in any family it's the responsibility of the older generations to pass along their values, traditions, stories, and faith to children. The youth worker's role is to help make that happen.

A youth mentoring program is one way to do it. What exactly is a mentoring program? Simply put, it's an attempt to *intentionally connect as many kids as possible with one or more adults who will get to know them, encourage them, and guide them toward adulthood.* In a sense it's an attempt to undo what the world has done and continues to do. While modern culture separates the young and the old and puts enmity between them, the church can bring adults and kids together.

To implement a mentoring program is in fact to participate in a holy act of reconciliation. Ironically many church youth ministries only reinforce the wall of division between the generations. When young people are isolated from the adults of the church, everybody loses. Not only do kids need adults, but adults need to recognize that they need young people. Churches without young people are dying churches. It serves no useful purpose to isolate the young people from the adults. Our kids need to be introduced to their spiritual relatives— brothers and sisters, grandparents, uncles, and aunts. By introducing a mentoring program, the church can become quite literally the extended family our young people never knew they had.

What Some Churches Are Doing

Shadow Mountain Community Church, El Cajon, California

Shadow Mountain Community Church is where my wife, Marci, and I direct a mentoring program that is now in its third year. Based largely on the principles and ideas that appear in the *One Kid at a Time* mentoring kit, which I co-authored with Miles McPherson,[6] this program has been designed to complement the existing youth ministry of the church, which is under the direction of youth pastors John Ruhlman and Ken Elben. (For more information on the senior high ministry of Shadow Mountain Community Church, see chapter 1 of this book. Most of the processes we use at Shadow Mountain to recruit and train mentors and to match them with young people is described in the "Making It Happen" section (p. 75).

Every week at Shadow Mountain, an announcement appears in the church bulletin inviting adults to "Join the M-Team" (The M-Team stands for mentor team, of course.) We also take advantage of other opportunities to recruit adults for the program. Our pitch includes the assurance that the adults aren't being asked to teach or to run any youth group activities, but simply to be friends to young people in the church. We invite prospective adults to one mentor training session (we hold several each year), at which time they not only receive some basic training in mentoring, but also are asked to commit themselves to become mentors for a period of at least one year.

After mentors have completed the training (either a one-day seminar or a series of three evening sessions), they are asked to fill out application forms and to submit themselves to fingerprinting and routine background checks. Then either they're on call to be matched with teenagers specially chosen for them, or they're invited to attend a youth ministry activity for the purpose of meeting kids and perhaps finding young people they would like to mentor. On occasion we plan a social event for young people and prospective mentors and let them pair off in a natural way.

Shadow Mountain's mentoring program is not highly regimented, nor is it high-profile. It exists largely in the background as a ministry performed by individuals who have caught the vision for caring about kids. Mentors, once they have been trained, are allowed the freedom to be creative in their mentoring relationships. We do our best to match them with teenagers either who have requested mentors or who have been brought to our attention by a parent or youth worker—but after that, they're pretty much on their own. We encourage mentors to meet with their kids as often as they can, greet them at church, call them on the phone from time to time, hang out with them, talk with them, pray with them, and just do what friends do.

The long-term goal of Shadow Mountain's mentoring program is to connect every young person in the church with one or more adults, but so far we have had to be content with a small but committed contingent of adults who are trying to make a difference with a few especially needy kids. In addition to the M-Team, we have dozens of other adults who are also involved in the youth ministry as volunteers, "platoon coaches," counselors, and Sunday school teachers, making them effective mentors as well. While the mentoring program at Shadow Mountain still has a long way to go, it has so far served as an effective way to gradually change the church's perception of youth ministry from something "someone else does" to something "we all do together."

Grace Christian Church, Warren, Michigan

Under the leadership of volunteer Danielle Bernock, the youth ministry of Grace Christian Church has for the past two years promoted its Adopt-a-Teenager program, which resembles a mentoring program but doesn't use that terminology. According to Bernock, the term "mentor" has the potential for turning off (or scaring off) adults who might think they're unqualified to be mentors.

Adopt-a-Teenager is designed to enlist adults who will agree to simply pray for individual young people in the church and to support them in other ways. Prior to enlisting these adults, the young people are surveyed to gather information about them (name, age, family background, school, interests). At that time, students are told what the Adopt-a-Teenager program is all about, and they are asked a number of questions regarding their preferences: Would you like to have someone praying for you on a regular basis? Would you like to know the name of your prayer partner? Would you mind having your prayer partner contact you, perhaps to find out what you would like him or her to pray for? Would you like to get to know your prayer partner as a friend?

The young people are then divided into four categories or "levels." The first level is "Just Pray for Me." There may be some teenagers who don't desire any contact with their prayer partners at all, but they do want others to pray for them. The second is "Let Me Know Who You Are." Unless a student requests this option, prayer partners are like "secret pals" who remain anonymous. Some kids prefer it that way. But if young people know who is praying for them, the door is open to deeper relationship. The third level is "Contact Is Fine." Young people who select this option are giving their prayer partners permission to call them or to otherwise make contact from time to time to share prayer requests or to just talk. The fourth level is "Yes, I Desire More Contact." Students who choose this option are inviting a deeper mentoring-type relationship with their adoptive adults, even though the term "mentoring" is rarely used.

Adults in the church are then given commitment forms, inviting them to indicate at which levels they would be willing to "adopt" young people. By doing so, they commit to following through with their responsibilities with the young people they're assigned based on the levels those young people prefer. For follow up, the young people are surveyed at least once a year to get feedback from them regarding the program. They're also asked to indicate the level at which they would like to continue in the program.

Moraga Valley Presbyterian Church, Moraga, California

Youth pastors Mike McLenahan and Jeff Haskel use mentoring in their church's confirmation program. Ordinarily confirmation occurs at early adolescence (junior high), but at Moraga Valley, it's reserved for high school students who are required to spend four months of intensive study learning the doctrines and creeds of the church.

Traditionally confirmation was the exclusive domain of the senior pastor (or another ordained minister) who taught the young people in a group setting—often with the unfortunate result of boring kids to death. As most youth workers know, *groups* of adolescents aren't always very attentive. But individually they can be surprisingly enthusiastic about learning the Bible and growing in their faith. For this reason, mentoring holds promise as an effective way to make confirmation a positive experience for kids rather than something to be endured.

At Moraga Valley, confirmation actually combines several elements. Students have "homework" (individual study), some teaching by the youth pastor in a group setting, plus the mentoring. Every young person is assigned an adult in the church—matched by personality, background, and skills—for a four-month period of time. They're required to meet at least five times. Specific exercises are provided for the mentoring pairs, including going to a "session" (church board) meeting together, visiting a mission that is supported by the church, and reading selected passages of Scripture together. The mentor serves not as a teacher, but as a companion and facilitator. Mentors at Moraga Valley are encouraged to make their mentoring experiences as enjoyable as possible for both themselves and the young people. They can invite the teenagers to their homes or their businesses, or they can spend some social times together. The young people learn from their mentors, but the mentors learn a lot as well.

Mike and Jeff have found that recruiting mentors for this program has been easy because (1) there is a relatively short time commitment and (2) there are specific, well-defined, task-oriented things to do. With this type of program, mentors know exactly what they're required to do, and they know exactly when they've completed the job. But in the process of mentoring young people for four months, they often find friends for life.

The Mennonite Church

I've been impressed with the mentoring program that has been incorporated for years into the youth ministries of many Mennonite churches. One of the salient features of this program is that mentoring is a rite of passage for young adolescents. Patterned after the example of Jesus, who was twelve when he left his mother and father and went to the temple to sit and learn from the elders (Luke 2:41-52), this program matches a young person with an adult mentor on his or her twelfth birthday.

But there are other reasons age twelve is appropriate for beginning a mentoring relationship. Lavon J. Welty writes, "Experience has shown that there is greater willingness to be matched with a mentor at this age when there are fewer school commitments and other involvements. As the youth gets further into high school and grows more and more busy with academics, extracurricular activities, sports, community involvements, and work, he or she will likely be more reluctant to enter into such a relationship."[7]

Given that modern society has robbed young adolescents of healthy rites of passage that mark their entrance into the adult world, a mentoring program that serves this function makes a lot of sense. In the Mennonite church, every young person is matched with an adult mentor and then confirmed before the entire congregation in a ritual ceremony. The mentor and the young person recite a pledge, committing themselves to the mentoring relationship for a specified period of time. They sign a mentoring covenant, and the pastor prays for the two of them as they begin their journey together. The parents and other family members stand with them, and their friends and the rest of the congregation serve as witnesses.

While such an approach to mentoring may not be practical for every church and every tradition, the concept of matching every young person with an adult mentor at a particular age or grade in school has a great deal of merit. There really is no better time to provide young people with adult mentors than on their entry into junior high or middle school.

Cathedral of the Valley, Escondido, California

Youth pastor Dan Daugherty had felt a need to begin a youth ministry mentoring program at his church for quite some time—matching young people one-on-one with adults. But after discussing the pros and cons—and the alternatives—of such a program with the church leadership, they decided to do something less risky and less difficult to administrate.

Besides working with the young people, Dan also serves his church as the "men's ministry" pastor. He implemented a program that is connecting men with boys. All the men of the church have been divided into small groups that meet weekly, and the boys from the youth group have been assigned to these groups. Every men's group is now responsible for particular boys who are part of their group. Dan is encouraging and teaching the men of the church how to influence the lives of young men, and giving them a way to do it through the church's small-group ministry.

Your Role in a Mentoring Program

As you can see, there are many different ways to implement a mentoring program in youth ministry. One thing they all have in common is a new role for the youth worker. Youth ministries of the past required the youth worker to be all things to all the kids—to do all the youth ministry all the time. But a vision for providing mentors for young people requires something different.

So if you want to start a mentoring program at your church, what will your role be? Actually, there are three. The first is to be "keeper of the vision." In a sense, this is something of a prophetic role. Just as the prophets of old tried to wake up the people of God with the truth, so the youth worker with a passion for effective youth ministry must articulate to the church a new way of thinking about youth ministry. Without a keeper of the vision—an advocate for young people who constantly reminds the church of its responsibility to the next generation—it is doubtful that anything will happen. If a mentoring program is going to have a chance at success, someone needs to be its champion, making it a priority on the church's agenda. That someone will probably be you.

Second, your role should be that of a trainer and encourager to mentors. This, I believe, is the primary role of today's professional youth worker. Like all leaders in the church, our first responsibility is to "equip the saints." We are to pass along what we know to others so that they can do what we do (2 Timothy 2:2). This is especially true for youth workers. You can't do it alone. Your job is to recruit and train other adults to love kids and to mentor them in the Christian faith—and then to be a cheerleader for those adults. Not only do they need equipping, but they also need encouraging. We must encourage mentors to hang in there and remind them how important they really are. Unless someone regularly and consistently does this, it's unlikely that mentors will last over the long haul.

Your third role is to become a mentor yourself. You will want to identify one or two kids you can mentor one-on-one. This may seem impossible if you were hired by the church to be a mentor for the entire youth group. But it's helpful to remember that even Jesus spent most of his time with just three disciples. Paul zeroed in on Timothy. Similarly, there are limits to how many young people you can effectively mentor. If you're doing youth ministry alone, you'll probably be accused of playing favorites, which is why it's so important to have a mentoring *team*. You can still direct the overall program, plan meetings and activities, and relate to the entire group as their leader. This is also important because it's difficult to recruit and train others to become mentors to individual kids unless you're doing it yourself. Out of your own mentoring relationships, you'll be able to lead by example and teach from experience.

Making It Happen

Let's turn our attention now to the "nuts and bolts" of getting a mentoring program up and running. If you follow the steps below, your chances of starting and maintaining an effective mentoring program are pretty good.

● DECIDE ON THE SCOPE OF THE PROGRAM. The first thing you need to do is assess how a mentoring program will fit into the existing programs of the church. For example, will your mentoring program replace the youth ministry program you have now, or will it be an addition to it? Will it be supported by other church staff members, particularly the senior pastor? Will there be any conflict with the adult ministries of the church or any others who are also recruiting volunteers? You'll need to carefully answer all these questions to avoid frustration and failure.

● BECOME A MENTOR YOURSELF. As I discussed above, it's important for you as a leader to enter into a mentoring relationship with one or more students before you try selling the program to others. Don't mentor someone just so you'll be able to look more authentic in the eyes of other people, though. My point here is simply this: Unless you yourself are a believer in mentoring and practice what you preach, there really is little chance that you'll be able to convince others of its value. The true test of whether you should begin a mentoring program is whether you're willing to be a mentor yourself.

● SET REALISTIC GOALS. Don't be overly ambitious, especially at first. One thing I've discovered is that mentoring is not an easy thing to sell to busy, overworked adults who already have too much to do. I have personally experienced the disappointment of seeing only five people show up for a mentor-training session out of a congregation of more than two thousand members. It's easy to become discouraged and judgmental when you don't get the kind of response you expect. But I've learned to appreciate the old adage, "Something is always better than nothing." I am always grateful for those five people who show up because that's potentially five more mentors than we had before. If I recruit and train five new mentors every six months, I'll have fifty mentors in five years!

● **DEFINE YOUR MENTORING PROGRAM.** Before you begin a mentoring program in your church, you'll need to be able to answer some important questions about the details of it. For example, who will administrate the program? Will it be you or someone else? In most cases, it's a good idea to have one specific "director of youth mentoring" who coordinates the program. Which students will be targeted for mentoring? junior high? senior high? church kids? unchurched kids? What will the mentors do?

In the mentoring kit *One Kid at a Time*, we recommend that mentors be recruited as either (1) friendship mentors, (2) vocational mentors, or (3) support mentors. Friendship mentors spend time with their kids one-on-one over an extended period of time. Vocational mentors invite students to learn about their occupations. Support mentors are like spiritual grandparents who pray for individual kids and remember them on special occasions. Think through all these details, and decide exactly what kind of program will be best for your church.

● **SHARE THE VISION AND BEGIN RECRUITING MENTORS.** Once you have defined your program, you can begin to share the vision for mentoring with the church at large. You'll want to take advantage of all the means at your disposal to do so. Make a presentation before the entire congregation. Have the students themselves invite adults to become their mentors. Put announcements in the church bulletin or church newsletter. Write letters to adults, or call them on the phone. You don't need to get firm commitments from people right away. Simply invite them to an initial mentor training session, where they can determine whether they want to be involved. Obviously this step is very important. Your mentoring program's success or failure will probably depend on how well you sell it to the congregation.

● **CONDUCT THE TRAINING SESSIONS.** Every mentor should receive training. The exact amount of training can vary depending on what you want your mentors to do, but three hours should be sufficient in most cases—at least to get them started. Martin Jacks, director of The Mentoring Center, believes mentoring programs should always be more concerned about recruiting quality mentors than about recruiting large numbers of them. "We recommend that mentoring programs make it difficult to become a mentor," he says. "Having a good heart is not enough. If someone doesn't have the patience to sit through three hours of training, he's [or she's] not going to have the patience to be a mentor."[8]

You can conduct one three-hour session or three one-hour sessions, depending on what's most convenient and practical. In the *One*

Kid at a Time mentoring kit, we offer three training sessions with an accompanying video. The first session defines mentoring, the second session deals with qualities of an effective mentor, and the third session answers the question "What does a mentor do?" It's important for you to take this opportunity to get acquainted with potential mentors and learn as much as you can about them. During the training sessions, mentors should also fill out application forms and be fingerprinted. (See the sample application form on pages 80-81.)

● CONFIRM EACH MENTOR. After mentors have completed the required training and filled out application forms, conduct personal interviews and background checks to assess the mentors' qualifications. I strongly recommend that you take this step seriously and follow through with the background checks on every mentoring candidate. You may know a person well and be very confident in their integrity and trustworthiness, but it's very important to keep complete files on everyone. In today's litigious climate, churches and organizations that fail to do background checks on the adults who work with children and young people may be found negligent if a mentor is ever accused of wrongdoing. Even though some expense is involved, it's smart to fingerprint everyone involved with youth (including yourself) and have those prints checked against the FBI's database of known sex offenders and pedophiles. While the chances of getting a bad report on someone are slim, this step reassures everyone that you have done your homework and haven't assumed anything.

The local authorities in your area can put you in touch with the appropriate agency for your particular state. There are all kinds of private investigative agencies that do background checks, but every state has a government agency that will release the same information at a lower cost. The name of the agency and the department under which it operates will vary from state to state, but one of the following should work for you: Department of Public Safety, State Bureau of Investigation, Criminal Justice Information Center, Crime Information Center, or State Police.

Once you've completed this process, you can confirm your mentors and let them know they'll soon be matched with kids.

● INVITE YOUNG PEOPLE TO PARTICIPATE. As the old saying goes "It takes two to tango." Not only do you need to share the vision for mentoring with adults and get your mentors trained and ready to go, but you also need to share the vision with your kids and invite them to be mentored by adults. Some kids will be reluctant to participate because they have misconceptions about mentoring. They may think mentoring is a plot by their parents to keep them in line. They may worry that mentors will make them do things they don't want to do or rob them of time with their friends. Most kids are understandably suspicious of adults, and it may be a real challenge to find ways to help them realize that they need mentors.

One of the best ways to share the concept of mentoring with kids is to speak to a group at a youth meeting or in some other setting, sharing stories of mentors in your life. You can explain to kids the advantages to having mentors. You may want to do a Bible study on mentoring or have some of the mentors-in-waiting come to the youth group and be introduced. I like to distribute response cards to the kids, and allow them to indicate their willingness to enter into mentoring relationships. If you present mentoring in a positive light, you will undoubtedly get a good response. You'll probably have more kids who want mentors than mentors available for them.

● **MATCH MENTORS WITH INDIVIDUAL KIDS.** As you might suspect, this is the trickiest part of the entire process. There is a certain amount of trial and error involved in matching young people with compatible adults. Sometimes the only way to find out is for mentors and kids to get together and see if they hit it off. I have planned social events for the purpose of bringing mentors and kids together informally. This allows some time to get acquainted, play games, and talk. Often some pairing-off happens naturally. In other cases, it might be best to simply use your best judgment and introduce the mentor to a young person you have chosen for him or her to mentor, and encourage the pair to get together a couple of times to see if they want to continue. Some mentoring programs allow kids to select mentors from among the adults they already know in the church. Regardless of how the matching process is done, don't take this step lightly. A great deal of care and thought needs to go into helping mentors get matched up with the right kids for them.

● **PROVIDE SUPPORT FOR YOUR MENTORS.** If a mentoring program is going to succeed, each mentor will need ongoing support and encouragement. One way to provide this is to schedule regular mentor-support meetings, perhaps on a monthly basis, so mentors can get together and share experiences, get further training, and pray together for the students they're mentoring. Another way is to personally contact each mentor on a regular basis to find out how things are going and to see if help is needed. Regular phone calls, letters, or even a newsletter can be very effective.

Regardless of what you do to support your mentors, the key to the long-term success of a mentoring program depends greatly on how the program is monitored and maintained. It's very easy for mentors to get discouraged or frustrated without letting you know. They may get busy and start feeling guilty because they aren't spending enough time with young people. They may have difficulties getting together with young people, or they may have other problems that interfere with mentoring relationships. Periodic phone calls or letters with a few words of encouragement can do wonders to keep mentors on the job and as effective as they can be.

It's Nothing New

Mentoring young people isn't a new concept. It's simply something we forgot how to do. As our lives have become busier and busier and as we have come to depend more and more on professionals for just about everything, we have forgotten that some things are best done "the old-fashioned way." Read Luke 2:41-52—the story of Jesus at age twelve who was separating from his parents and beginning his transition into adulthood. There he sat in the temple, surrounded not by kids, but by adults. Even Jesus needed mentors.

(For more information on how to implement mentoring in youth ministry, see *Intensive Caring: Practical Ways to Mentor Youth* and *Successful Youth Mentoring*, both published by Group Publishing, Inc.)

Application to Be a Mentor

We appreciate your interest in becoming a mentor. Mentors are concerned adults who commit their time, skill, and creativity to help young people achieve their potential through consistent relationship. The information in this application will help us match you with a young person and will be kept confidential.

Date: _____

Name: _____

Ethnic origin: (Please circle)

African American   Hispanic   Caucasian   Asian   Other

Street address: _____

City: _____ State: _____ ZIP: _____

Phone: (H) _____ (W) _____ Pager: _____

Marital Status:

___ Married to first spouse	___ Never married	___ Divorced
___ Divorced & remarried	___ Separated	___ Widowed
___ Widowed & remarried		

Spouse's name (if applicable): _____

Child(ren)'s name(s) and age(s) (if applicable): _____

_____

Occupation: _____ Employer: _____

Birth date: _____ Gender: _____ Age: _____

Languages (other than English): _____

Would you agree to have us check your name through federal and state criminal records of child abuse and neglect proceedings? (Please circle)   Yes   No

Social Security Number:_____

Please list any special interests, skills, hobbies, or areas of expertise where you feel you can be of help. _____

_____

_____

Please list examples of any prior volunteer experience. _____

_____

Please circle words that describe your personality.

Spiritual	Sensitive	Quiet	Outgoing
Adventuresome	Happy	Shy	Talkative
Confident	Moody	Nervous	Friendly
Enthusiastic	Impatient	Impulsive	Serious
Good-natured	Assertive	Bold	Cheerful

Other: _____

List three people who can serve as character references for you.

Name: _____ Address _____
City: _____ State: _____ ZIP: _____
Phone: _____ Relationship: _____

Name: _____ Address: _____
City: _____ State: _____ ZIP: _____
Phone: _____ Relationship: _____

Name: _____ Address: _____
City: _____ State: _____ ZIP: _____
Phone: _____ Relationship: _____

Please list one work reference:

Name: _____ Address: _____
City: _____ State: _____ ZIP: _____
Phone: _____ Relationship: _____

As a mentor, you would be asked to make the following commitments:

● Commit to working with at least one young person for at least one year with the possibility of continuing the relationship on a long-term basis.

● Commit to maintaining weekly contact with your teenager(s) and to meet face to face at least once a week for a period of one to three hours.

● Commit to completing mentor training before being matched with a teenager.

● Commit to regular supervision and evaluation.

● Commit to assisting your teenager in identifying and achieving academic, personal, and spiritual goals.

● Commit to basing your relationship on respect for the teenager and his or her family.

I certify that the information I have supplied is correct to the best of my knowledge. I grant permission to contact the references provided and to complete a background check.

Signature: _____ Date: _____

ENDNOTES

1. Jean Houston, "The Initiation of Telemachus," *Crossroads: The Quest for Contemporary Rites of Passage* (Chicago and La Salle, IL: Carus Publishing Company, 1996), 35.

2. *1994 Annual Report of the International Youth Foundation* (Battle Creek, MI: International Youth Foundation, 1994), 7.

3. Urie Bronfenbrenner, "What Do Families Do?" Family Affairs (Institute for American Values, 1991), 33.

4. From a poll of 758 children and adolescents between the ages of ten and seventeen, along with their parents, commissioned by Newsweek magazine and the Children's Defense Fund and published in Newsweek, November 22, 1993, pages 52-53. Respondents were asked who has a "very important" influence on them (or, for parents, who influenced them when they were their children's age). Children and adolescent responses: 86 percent, parents; 56 percent, grandparents; 55 percent, place of worship; 50 percent, teachers; 41 percent, peers; 23 percent, community organizations; 22 percent, media. Parent responses: 81 percent, parents; 47 percent, grandparents; 55 percent, place of worship; 48 percent, teachers; 37 percent, peers; 17 percent, community organizations; 20 percent, media.

5. "The Second Birth Called Adolescence: A Conversation with H. Stephen Glenn," Youthworker (Winter 1994), 65.

6. Miles McPherson with Wayne Rice, *One Kid at a Time: How Mentoring Can Transform Your Youth Ministry* (Colorado Springs, CO: David C. Cook, 1995).

7. Lavon J. Welty, *Side by Side: Mentoring Guide for Congregational Youth Ministry* (Newton, KS: Faith and Life Press, 1989), 37.

8. "Mentoring Mania Hits Oakland," *Youth Today* (March/April 1997), p. 13.

CHAPTER 5:
Going Beyond the Stained Glass Curtain

Ministering to the Community
Through Community Cooperation

JOHN R. CUTSHALL
Youth Minister at First Christian Church in Marshall, Illinois

A Story

Once upon a time, a community of people started out on a great quest together. All was going well until they came to a great chasm. This chasm presented a problem to everyone in the community, and they were greatly saddened. Then the thinkers in the community arose and spoke in mighty words, saying, "If we use a springboard, which by luck we have, we can cross this great chasm." And a cheer arose from the community! Then one of the wise ones set his springboard, tested his calculations, and made his leap—only to miss the far side of the chasm and fall to his death.

Then another group in the community arose—those who boasted of great physical strength. Massive were their muscles, and poor was their English. "We don't need no stinking springboard machines," they said. "We can do it through our own strength." And a cheer arose from the community! Then one of the strong ones flexed his muscles, stretched his limbs, and made his leap—only to miss the far side of the chasm and fall to his death.

Then another group in the community arose. This group was full of mighty and wild cheers, and they said, "With excitement and enthusiasm we can cross any chasm we face. We must be positive in our attitudes! Let us cheer together, and the strength of our spirit will lift us across." And there was great cheering and shouting and clamor. And the community cheered into the night and awoke the next morning exactly where they had been the night before.

At this point, some despaired. Without a solution, they simply leaped into the great chasm and perished.

Then one arose and said, "Let us gather our wits and our resources." The community looked around and spied a tree of massive size. The wise ones calculated that it would span the chasm. Those who boasted of physical might began to chop and cut at the base of the tree, but they quickly tired. Then those of great enthusiasm and excitement arose and cheered. Soon those of great strength were refreshed by the cheers, and they felled the mighty tree so that the whole community could walk across its mighty trunk to the other side of the chasm. Thus the community on a quest learned that only by working together could they conquer the obstacles they faced.

Is it only a simple little story, or could it hold a moral for those in youth ministry today?

Some Really Deep Thoughts

If there is a constant in youth ministry, it's that the applications of youth ministry continue to change. The message doesn't, but the way we deliver it does. In nearly twenty years of youth ministry, I've filled shelves with resources and put together files of events, but most of them can't be unboxed or unshelved and used without major reworking. Youth culture has changed since that old program last saw the light of day. Why should we waste time trying to reach young people the same way we did in the last few decades?

What hasn't changed is the desire of the church to influence the world with the good news of Christ. Our goal is to touch teenagers, their families, and our communities with God's love. That has always been the core of the gospel. Today's youth ministers must work in such a way that entire communities are influenced by the ministry God works through them and their churches.

"Influence," as defined by Webster's, is the "power to affect others," and that is exactly what God has given us (Acts 1:8). We've been given the Holy Spirit, who empowers us to influence our communities and the entire world.

For centuries that's exactly what the church did. Christians influenced music, art, government, and communities for years until the mid-1900s,[1] when something changed. For many reasons the church was told to take a back seat, and we obeyed. We lost much of our influence in the arts, literature, government, schools, and our communities. The good news is that the winds have changed, and once again people are looking to the church as an agent of influence in our communities.

What has changed? As far as the laws and the government are concerned, that depends on which lawyer you listen to. The courts continue to argue over what the church can and cannot do in federal institutions and schools. It's become a national sport. The laws bounce back and forth like Ping-Pong balls, and sometimes they bounce our way.

Whatever the laws regarding schools and federal institutions, though, the church is free to move as an equal partner in plenty of other areas. People in all sorts of groups are looking for the kind of assistance and influence you have to give. There are numerous clubs, organizations, and gatherings that have access to young people and need what you and your church have to give.

The church is no longer barred from the outside, and churches who choose to emerge from their own walls are finding new avenues of influence in the community outside the "stained glass curtain." But the doors of the church have to be unlocked from the inside. If you approach the community in an attitude of cooperation and accessibility, the church can influence society and gain an ear for what we have to offer.

Gaining an ear is the key. We can no longer assume that people want to or will listen to us; we must discover ways to prove that the church has a message that can add value to the community just as we did in the first century. This is truly a call back to our roots.

So if the community accepts the church as an equal partner, it's up to the church to step up to the challenge and become the influencer it was intended to be all along. Jesus called us to be salt in this world. Remember, the function of salt is to add flavor to what is already there. We can come alongside community clubs, service groups, and organizations to partner with them for a better world. "This community-based perspective allows us to see how families, schools, peers, media, businesses, religious organizations, and other forces all influence the lives of young people."[2]

The Uninspired Beginning of an Inspired Concept

We had driven a couple of hours to attend a drug-prevention seminar in another town. When we got there, we realized that more than half of the audience was from our hometown. At least four different agencies had driven separate cars and had all assumed no one else in our community was interested in driving all that way. As we laughed about the situation, someone said, "Wouldn't it be nice if all the youth-oriented agencies could get together and talk? Even if it only meant we could share rides to events like this." With that inspired casual comment, the concept of the Marshall Area Youth Network (MAYN) began its journey from theory to reality.

A week after the seminar, a small group of community leaders met to discuss the feasibility of meeting together on a regular basis to share resources and information so that all the agencies involved could benefit. We had bundles of questions: Is it possible for schools, courts, law enforcement agencies, human resource counselors, social workers, state and federal government workers, and churches to work together as equals? What can we do to bridge all our philosophical differences as well as pragmatic and systematic differences? What have others tried? How do we handle the egos of so many leaders in the same room? What kind of results can we expect? Are there goals on which we can agree? Are there legalities and/or prejudices we need to overcome?

It has taken awhile, but we've found that state agencies, judicial offices, schools, community clubs and organizations, law enforcement, and churches can work together, and all become winners in the process. The benefits of us working together have produced a whole lot more than a ride-share program.

What We Have Become

MAYN has functioned for four years and has broken many of the barriers that had previously plagued our community. Our monthly meetings include discussions about young people, youth culture, the specific youth culture in our town, and projects that involve our members. Youth workers find that they aren't alone in their struggles to reach young people, and they find resources, programs, encouragement, and people available that they never knew existed.

The adventure of networking has given us many successes. There have been times when someone has needed a speaker and another member of MAYN has been able to step into that position or to find someone who could. At one time, an organization called to complain to us because they hadn't been specifically invited to a community meeting. They later explained that they were frustrated because they couldn't find a place to donate a sum of money they had collected. MAYN offered assistance, and the problem was solved to the benefit of everyone.

Cooperation has allowed us to see organizations as people, not banners or stereotypes. It has opened lines of communication and allowed people to link together to become more than they were by themselves. In itself, MAYN is not a religious organization, nor is it anti-religious. It has no political agenda and is not an entity that functions to bring any power to bear on any of its member organizations. It is a neutral meeting place where civic organizations, clubs, and agencies work together to help young people. The fact that churches are involved as equal partners with other members isn't seen as a threat or a problem by the other members.

There are very few limits and many benefits to what a cooperative can do for your community and specifically your church. It takes time and willingness to assist others to get things started. But if you have a desire to get things started, that's one of the contributions you bring to the mix. The community cooperative is a way for the church to gain an ear and an audience for another more important message, the gospel of Christ. You may even be surprised at what you'll learn.

But where to begin...

Start by Identifying Youth-Focused Organizations

How many youth-focused organizations do you have in your community? How many groups would list "character development of young people" as a high priority? Have you ever asked? Finding these organizations is a lot easier than you may think. Break out your telephone book. Look under "youth," "clubs," or "agencies." You can also ask schools, teenagers, and coaches what organizations and activities are sponsored for the young people in your community. Make your list, and while you're at it, include the name and phone number of each leader.

Once you have a list— even an incomplete list—you'll need to find a place to meet. Churches are designed as meeting places and offer excellent facilities. Contact the organizations on your list, and describe the vision of networking around the concept of shared resources and information. You may not get everyone to participate, but you may be surprised at who shows up.

Don't get discouraged if you run into a no or a no-show—some organizations may be wary of a hidden agenda. And not everyone will be able to work together on all projects. For example, Lions Clubs focus on children's eyesight while you may want to focus on strengthening the family, but in some areas you can work together. Shoot for the common goals, and expand from there.

Find a person with the spiritual gift of telephoning. Create a form that outlines the basics of the cooperative and includes a place to record information about organizations (name, president, purpose, annual activities, contact person and phone number, resources they can share or barter). (See the sample below.) You can mail out these forms, but the return rate will be slow. Phone calls will be worth the extra time.

It will take time, but get together with an officer from every organization you can. Seek to understand their goals and their purposes, then paint the vision of cooperation. Many times you'll find that organizations are looking for great causes to support. And many of them will tell you a minister has never sought to understand what they're trying to do.

Create a directory of youth organizations. This may be as simple as photocopying the forms you've filled out on the phone and stapling them together. Or you may want to put the information on a computer

---

Name of organization: _____

Address: _____

City: _____ State: _____ ZIP: _____

Name of contact person: _____

Phone: (_____) _____-_____

Officer(s): _____

Short description of the organization's purpose: _____

_____

_____

Activities: _____

_____

_____

Resources to share or trade with others: _____

_____

_____

and print it out. This will give you something to offer those who come to your first few meetings. You'll be surprised at how many resources and opportunities you have just created for yourself and your youth group. And you'll be surprised at the new information you receive when people realize their organizations aren't included in your directory.

Learn a New Vocabulary

As church members, some of our speech has become unique to the church. We "fellowship" instead of "get together," we "disciple" instead of "mentor," we do a lot of things other people do, but we call them by names other people don't understand. "Christianese" has become so much a part of the way Christians speak that it takes some effort to learn a new language.

Being a youth minister, I thought I wasn't affected by church-speak. Communication with the outside world was a normal thing for me and wouldn't be a problem. I found it interesting, though, that when I would get excited about a topic in a MAYN meeting, others would wrinkle their foreheads in confusion. Finally a light would come on, and someone would explain that they used a different term for what I was describing. I found out that other organizations have similar inbred speech patterns. When you experience a breakthrough in communication or when you don't understand an acronym, write it down. Learn the languages of others, and you'll find acceptance as you seek to understand.

Survey Influencers

You've heard the old adage "Work smarter and not harder." The amazing thing about influencers is that they do both. They work smarter and harder. You've probably heard the Pareto Principle:[3] Twenty percent of the things you do result in 80 percent of your success. And 80 percent of the things you do result in only 20 percent of your success. It's true! Twenty percent of your teenagers take 80 percent of your time. You may have a closet full of clothes, but you wear 20 percent of those clothes 80 percent of the time. Why else would you stand in front of your closet and say, "I have nothing to wear."

Your goal is to identify the influencers in your community and your local student body and to find ways to work with them. Who sets the pace, creates the attitudes, and makes the rules? Who could start a wave of positive peer (youth or adult) pressure that would change your community as you know it?

MAYN struggled for a long time before realizing that it wasn't only the student council or the peer counselors who wielded the power of leadership. To be honest we weren't quite sure who the leaders were when it came to the young people in our community. So we asked. We went to the local school system and asked permission to give out a simple questionnaire. We defined what we meant by influencer, and we asked two very simple questions: Who are the top two teenage influencers in your life? and Who are the top two adult influencers in your life? We collected the surveys and tallied the results. Those who received numerous votes were listed as influencers.

To our surprise, and with some discomfort, we found a cross-section of all kinds of teenagers from all walks of life. We had the "brains" and the "bands," the "dopers" and the "jocks." We found the "goths" and the "hackers." All along, most of us had hoped it was the "honor rollers" that carried the influence, but what we found was that we needed to reach out and recognize that the members of the "detention hall of fame" were just as influential in their own ways.

We discovered that among adults, parents held the number-one spot and teachers held the number-two position. Especially strong were coaches and teachers who were with teenagers outside the classroom in supervising extracurricular activities.

The influential teenagers were a true 20 percent of the kids. It confirmed the Pareto Principle. These young people we had identified set the pace for the other 80 percent of the student body. And we had a true cross-section of youth culture.

As the Marshall Area Youth Network discussed our results, we decided to discreetly focus on the 20 percent influencers, and let them influence the other 80 percent without stretching our time and energies beyond reasonable boundaries. In essence, we narrowed the focus of our target audience and yet broadened our sphere of influence.

We targeted the teenagers and the adults for special encouragement. The people who share their lives and open their hearts to teenagers deserve all the encouragement we can muster. You don't have to be a great organization to offer great awards. Who is the American Music Academy anyway? We created our own coveted award and gave it away with plenty of fanfare.

We targeted these influencers for special-awareness training. Most of the influencers had no idea they were as effective as they really were. Parents never believe they're as influential as they are, and with all the pressures teachers face daily, survival seems to top their list of priorities.

We also brought these people together for mind-mapping (a form of brainstorming) sessions. If these people were doing it right, we figured we should get their opinions on what needed to be done in the future. We wanted to be pragmatic and study what was working, then go out and duplicate it. The great thing is that many of the answers we were looking for were in our own back yard. All we had to do was identify them and put them to work.

> **MIND MAPPING**
>
> Mind mapping is a brainstorming technique that uses the association of words and ideas to come up with new ideas. To make a mind map, start in the center of a page with your main idea, then work outward from there in every direction, clustering associated ideas and words together. Every item then becomes potentially the center of another map. Visual memory is an important aspect of mind mapping— using color, symbols, icons, 3-D effects, arrows, and other visual features to help people remember what they see.

The Town Meetings

We knew that the teenager survey was just a beginning and couldn't be an end unto itself. MAYN called open town meetings. These meetings introduced us to the community and helped us establish some credibility as an organization that wanted to listen. By talking with business and community leaders, we found out very quickly where young people stood as a priority in our community.

We learned that a luncheon was an excellent format to gather busy people. Even busy people have to eat! And we were professional enough not to take more time than necessary. Rather than simply zooming in on single segments of society, we decided to pull back to a wide-angle view and examine how our whole community impacted our young people, both positively and negatively.[4] We gleaned information and then boiled it down into usable components and shared it with the people who helped make it possible. Leaders who at first were wary, soon warmed up to the idea of cooperation when they discovered that it helped them accomplish their goals.

Multiplying the Bottom Line

Some of the MAYN organizations had been sponsoring two teenagers to attend a leadership convention each year. One specific summer, the teenagers returned with some discouraging stories. Was the community's money being used in the most effective way? Were the teenagers learning what we wanted them to learn? After this problem was presented at our monthly meeting, we decided we could present our own leadership training for the same amount of money and focus in on the topics that affected our local teenagers.

The first thing we did was ask the teenagers what they wanted included in a leadership-training day. They came up with twelve topics, including the predictable: drugs, abuse, teenage sexuality, and self-esteem. But there were a few topics that caught us by surprise. We ran across questions such as "How do I get everything done? (which led to a discussion on time management); "What do I do when my best friend becomes a dad?" and "What happens when my parents are doing drugs?"

Your topics will differ from ours because your teenagers are different from the teenagers we work with in our community. But the process of gathering the information will help your group come to terms with the young people in your area. And in the minds of the teenagers, it will put you in the small percentage of adults who listen to them. This recognition alone is worth the time investment.

After processing the information the teenagers gave us, we looked at our resources. What money had we been spending on the regional convention? What speakers were available? What dates were available to us? We asked a lot of questions and struggled with the answers. The struggle again cemented us together as a working unit that now owned the information, rather than just a doughnut-dunking social group that discussed national trends and how we thought they might impact our teenagers.

Our leadership day, Take Charge, emerged as a one-day training event on a school holiday. We publicized and preregistered, and one-fourth of the high school students came to school on their day off to learn how to better their lives. It was a success in every way. Not only did we multiply the use of the money entrusted to us, but we got to grapple with issues that were real in the lives of the teenagers in our community. The teenagers appreciated us listening to them as much as the presentations made during the "Take Charge" event. Instead of just two, there were now scores of teenagers who could talk about the message that was presented. And even the press sang our praises as the TV and newspaper coverage marveled at the magic of getting that many teenagers in one place on a day off from school without a single discipline problem. Through cooperation, all the MAYN organizations were there to interact with the teenagers. We worked as a team, and we won!

Celebrate the Family

One of the goals of MAYN is promoting strong family units. We had lamented that it was the parents who really didn't need to attend that attended all the parenting seminars that any of our organizations offered. In an attempt to reach the families that were more difficult to reach, we decided to sponsor a day to emphasize the importance of the family. We called it "Celebrate the Family."

We contacted city leaders and reserved the fairgrounds. Recreation areas donated the use of swimming pools, bowling alleys, and golf courses to the cause, and churches taught and preached on the importance of the family. The first year we had more than 10 percent of our community turn out to join our celebration. In the years that followed, per MAYN's suggestion, many of the churches gave up their regular Sunday morning worship services for a joint service at the fairgrounds.

I'm not saying that one day a year is going to work a miracle and put all our families back together. But sometimes the reward isn't measured in numbers or in the information you can get into the hands of the people. Sometimes success is seeing families laugh, swim, shoot hoops, and worship together. That all happened at Celebrate the Family, and it was because a group of leaders had already committed to work together for the common good.

The Homework Club

At one of our meetings, someone introduced the idea of helping young people academically. After much discussion, we came up with the idea of starting a homework club. One of the agencies in MAYN wrote a grant to provide the funds to support it. Junior high students soon found a warm and caring place they could go after school for tutoring, cookies, and an understanding smile.

All was well until the grant ran out. We discovered that we needed a different source of funding. Eventually we found a new source of funding, and the homework club continues to be a bright spot in the lives of many junior high students.

Communication and Cooperation, Resources and Relationships

These success stories are just the tip of the iceberg when it comes to the benefits of starting a youth-focused cooperative. MAYN has been able to discuss and deal with issues from community health to parent-teenager relationships to vandalism. We get cards and calls from teenagers who thank us for challenging them and preparing them for life. MAYN focuses on groups but never forgets that individuals change individuals. And just by being available and aware, you can change lives.

Magazine articles follow newspaper articles confirming that problems such as drug abuse, alcohol abuse, gangs, and teenage violence are community problems that communities need to address. We've found ourselves ahead of problems because of the relationships built around MAYN.

The relationships are an advantage in themselves. Professionals not only find a network of resources, they also build trust with other professionals who want them to succeed. There is no need for walls of personal or professional separation because even if they disagree on the ways to reach goals, at least some of their goals are the same.

Relationships with teenagers and families are another bonus. Cooperative members are called upon to present keynote addresses and chaperone events that other organizations are sponsoring. (It's true; the church isn't the only place that needs volunteer help.) You can pitch in simply as a parent or a concerned member of the community. Your congregation will be surprised (and pleased) to see you at a scout outing or as a special speaker at a women's tea. The community needs what you have to give. The problem may be finding out what you have to give to the relationships around you, and letting other people know that you're willing to be there for them.

Look at What You Have to Give!

At times church workers get too wrapped up in their own schedules, victories, and failures to see the big picture. This is just human nature for the most part, but there must come a time when you realize that the community is starving for what you've been trained to do!

People need the expertise you have in leading small groups and discussions. They're looking for people who have experience in getting young people involved and then debriefing to help them discover what they've learned. Some clubs and organizations are looking for special speakers and programs that either speak to young people directly or to parents and other youth workers about the youth culture in your community.

These are your areas of experience and expertise. The fact that you can offer them to the community allows you to see and to be seen beyond the stained glass walls. You'll be viewed as a leader who cares about more than just your own personal or church goals. And if you have a performance talent such as singing, comedy, or clowning, you'll have people begging you to come.

You and your church have much to offer the community, even if it's just a room to meet in and a good coffee pot. Sit down and list those resources, and spread the news that you're willing and trained to help others succeed.

How to Start

Starting MAYN was a group effort that has developed and taken on the characteristics of our community. This will be true with your youth network as you begin the process. And though there are many ways you can start, let me list a few things we've learned along the way.

● *Identify youth-focused organizations, clubs, and agencies in your community.*

This is a must, and we've covered this in detail, but the more people you contact with your vision, the more people will join you in the effort. This is a vital step, and one that continues as you and your core group evolve.

● *Set up a vision-setting meeting.*

Getting people together is the name of the game. Find a place that's large enough and that has the facilities for refreshments. Adults, like teenagers, love food and are more relaxed when it's available.

● *Establish a mission statement.*

If you can put the goals of your network into a sentence, you'll be able to share that vision with more people. A constitution is good and a manifesto is impressive, but a simple goal statement will allow you to all start and remain on the same page.

● *Keep your meetings to a consistent length.*

You're asking busy people who hold important roles in their organizations to give up time they could be using elsewhere to come to your meeting. You'll need to keep the meetings to a consistent length so they can and will schedule you in. Even if you're in the middle of a very lively discussion, it's better to schedule another special meeting to finish it than to go into a two- or three-hour marathon session. Leaders see this as a betrayal of trust and an imposition on their time.

● *Find a facilitator or two and not a leader who dominates.*

If you or any member of your group dominates the discussion, you'll kill it. This is a cooperative, and all members come to it on a level playing field. This must be clear from the beginning. When "team" becomes the goal, the results will be much richer than if one individual decides to fly off on an ego trip.

● *Find a big project and make it a top priority.*

By finding a big project you can all work on together, you'll find that each group member takes ownership of the network. It will become *our* network and not *your* network or *the* network. Finding a *big* project allows your group to prove to itself that it can accomplish more as a group than its members could as individual organizations. Another bonus is that you can get the attention of the press, and the community will begin to recognize the network by name.

● *Let the community in on the secret.*

Remember that you're on a treasure hunt, and treasure isn't always lying around on the ground in plain sight. You'll have to dig for the real successes, and to do that you need publicity. Let the newspapers and the radio stations in on what you're doing. Find an artist who is willing to create an easy-to-identify logo. Let your humility show through your willingness to give praise to the other organizations, and you'll find that your influence will grow proportionately.

● *Ask the tough questions.*

Kudos and Brownie points are good from time to time, but remember you're trying to reach the youth of your community. Don't be afraid to ask the tough questions and to try what hasn't been tried before. What has worked in your community before? What hasn't worked? Remember, you may be dealing with other people's egos and pet projects. How do you deal with people in influential positions who are bad role models? What's the best way to deal with sex, drugs, and rock 'n' roll? Can churches be treated with equality in a group of community organizations and clubs? Does God have a place in your community? These questions are tough and can create some intense discussions, but your network has amassed more people and more talent than have ever been gathered before in your community. You have resources and the knowledge to make a difference. Take heart, gather your courage, and start tackling the giants that stand between you and a better community.

I've Got the Recipe, but Where's the Oven?

There are few models of youth ministry that really cook. This one does. It allows the church to be the salt and the light it was intended to be without boycotting, protesting, or preaching from the street corner. People get to see the church and your youth ministry for the caring, loving outreach it truly is. The recipe for influence is simply a matter of finding the needs of the larger community and adding the ingredients of other community clubs, organizations, and churches.

But as with any recipe, the temperature of the oven affects the taste it leaves in your mouth. The community cooperative model is best served in areas where people are warm to the idea of helping young people. No matter how you cut it, a cooperative means finding common ground and working together. Too much heat from too many areas might burn you and the cooperative.

But if a hot issue has just passed through a community, people are often more open to forming a task force or a cooperative. This is a great temperature in which to rise to the occasion. Even if some people in your community seem cold to your ideas, remember that one organization or one individual doesn't a community make. Seek out those who are willing to get into the kitchen, discuss recipes, and start cooking.

Legal Ramifications

There is an anxiety that looms over the church when it comes to getting involved in community organizations and school systems in particular. It stems from the ever-boiling controversy between church and state. There are many books and other resources out there that deal with this issue in ways I can't. Let me just say that you as a member of the community can and should take part in the direction your town or city is going. You have expertise regarding young people and youth culture that's valuable to your community, and if you're invited to be a part of a network or an organization, you should be free to be there as a guest or a leader. I recommend the following resources that deal with this issue more directly:

● J.W. Brinkley with K.C. Crump, *Students' Legal Rights on a Public School Campus,* Roever Communications, P.O. Box 136130, Fort Worth, TX 76136.

● www.rutherford.org. Homepage of the Rutherford Institution. They deal with religious freedoms and the law on a daily basis.

● www.religious-freedom.org. A nondenominational homepage with information on the latest laws that affect church and state.

Maybe...

Maybe your community is on a quest to better itself. Maybe your church or your youth ministry is looking for a way to influence the youth culture that immediately surrounds your church building. You don't need flash; you just want good, solid answers to the questions that surround today's young people.

"It's becoming increasingly clear that, just as every institution may be in some way responsible for our current situation, no segment of society can single-handedly turn it around. No one alone is in a position to address the needs or create the kind of support, values, and competencies young people need to grow up healthy."[5]

Maybe the answer, as far as the church is concerned, is our desire. Many churches look outside the confines of their walls, and what they see scares them: "I would love to minister to the entire community, but I feel overwhelmed with the church as it is. Where do I get the volunteers, the resources, and the finances to launch a community-wide ministry? What would my people say?"

These and other fears have been enough to keep the church timid in its attempts to step out, to learn the language of our society, and to minister to communities. We keep assuring ourselves that Christ will provide the answers. Maybe Christ has already provided the answers to many of our problems in the communities that surround our churches. And maybe he is waiting on us to respond. Just maybe...

ENDNOTES

1. In McCollum vs. Board of Education, 333 U.S. 203 (1948), the court found religious instruction in public schools a violation of the establishment clause and therefore unconstitutional. In Engel vs. Vitale, 370 U.S. 421 (1962), the court found school prayer unconstitutional.

2. Dr. Dale A. Blyth with Eugene C. Roehlkepartain, *Healthy Communities, Healthy Youth* (Minneapolis, MN: Search Institute, 1993), 7.

3. John C. Maxwell, *Developing the Leader Within You* (Nashville, TN: Thomas Nelson Publishers, 1993).

4. Blyth and Roehlkepartain, *Healthy Communities, Healthy Youth,* 5.

5. Blyth and Roehlkepartain, *Healthy Communities, Healthy Youth,* 7.

CHAPTER 6:
Finding a Lost Generation

Ministering Through a Youth Church

CATHI BASLER
Co-Director of Souled Out Ministries in Mt. Prospect, Illinois

Worlds Apart

You've probably noticed the kids hanging around the local convenience store or your favorite mall. They dress in all sorts of extreme styles, they smoke, they go to all the parties, they have drinking problems, and they've probably tried the latest drug. You might even read about them in the newspaper. By the time they're sixteen, they've had plenty of relationships, probably tried sex, maybe even had a child. They're on every street and sidewalk in America—across the world, for that matter.

Sure, they've heard God's name. They probably say it more than you do. But they don't go to church, even on Christmas and Easter. Why would they? Many of them don't even know what Christmas and Easter mean. MTV sells them its own brand of theology.

A vast percentage of today's young people belong to an unreached people group—an unreached generation. They have absolutely no idea that God adores them and wants to let them know how much he cares.

Then there are the Christian kids who've basically grown up in church. They go to church, hang out with all the right people, get good grades, and gossip only sometimes. They show up at youth group and attend sports functions. They know God loves them, and they're pretty sure their parents do too. They don't talk to the other kids much. They can't. They aren't supposed to hang out with kids like that, and besides, they don't know how. These two groups of kids have almost nothing in common—maybe an occasional gym class, but that's about it.

Most Christian youth programs are reaching primarily the Christian kids. But if the kids don't even mix at school, how can we ask them to mix at church? And why would a teenager who has never stepped foot in a church come to youth group anyway?

Our Story

When our own children became teenagers and started to bring their friends home, my husband and I began to ask ourselves how we could reach those kids. We both had become Christians as teenagers and knew what an incredible difference that choice had made in the course of our lives. Many of our kids' friends had never heard that they could have a personal relationship with Jesus Christ. So we really wanted to share God's love with them.

We hosted a youth group in our home. One night when we had dozens of kids in our home, the kids played the raisin-up-your-nose game. After that night none of those unchurched kids ever came back again. After that, we found ourselves wondering how programs like that would significantly reach the young people of today. When we started looking, it seemed as if everywhere we looked, there were hurting young people.

God began to open our eyes and our hearts to teenagers. He gave us a deep burden for prayer. It wasn't unusual for us to go to the local mall and find ourselves weeping, asking God to help us reach these unreachable kids. We knew that to reach this generation would take more than silly games.

We watched our own children begin to feel left out in their schools. They knew that to do what the other kids did would be against what they believed, but not to would make them outcasts. We searched for ways to bring kids together, for a place they could hang out together. But we didn't find any place. So we started a youth group in our home without games. We invited our kids' friends from school and kids from the Sunday school class we taught. It was a slow start, but the youth group grew. Soon we faced a new problem.

One Wednesday Night

One Wednesday evening as the cars were beginning to line our street, our pastors came to talk. They had come to discuss the future of the youth group that was filling our home. We had been working with the group for more than a year. It had grown and attracted kids who had never even stepped foot in church, along with those who had come from our Sunday school class.

One of our pastors' concerns was how this group fit in with our church youth program. Why were dozens of kids coming who had never attended any of our church services? As we talked, the young people grew louder on the other side of the hallway. Outside the front door, the smokers claimed their traditional spots by the "butt can." The kids who came—with their multi-colored hair and body piercings—hardly looked like the young people of our church. Our pastors sat in our living room and looked at us with dismay, not wanting our church kids to be negatively influenced, yet aware that it was God who was drawing the kids to our home.

My husband and I shared our dreams for this generation of young people, asking them to help us reach out to the kids. But our pastors didn't know what to make of this. Both men were unable to stay for the youth meeting. As they left, our assistant pastor looked at us with tears in his eyes, telling us he just couldn't see how both our visions could fit together. "How do you mix church kids with kids who have never walked into a church?" he asked.

"How do you not?" I cried.

As they left, the kids kept coming. That night our home was full of dozens of teenagers from various high schools, most coming for the first time to hear a message of love and forgiveness from a God they did not know. At the beginning of that meeting, our hearts were heavy. We knew we would have to break from our church of over seventeen years. Yet as we looked on the faces of the desperate teenagers, we knew there was no turning back.

A Youth Church

From the seeds of that night, our youth church was born. Every Thursday night, young people from junior high to college age converge on our building, The Heart & Soul Café, for our service. As the parking lot fills up, our student leaders greet newcomers and have them fill out guest cards. The coffee bar is open, and some of the kids play pool.

At 8:00 p.m. the lights dim, smoke fills the room, and the band begins to play. Colored lights and strobes flash as the meeting is announced. Some of the kids who came just to hang out in the parking lot decide to stumble into what is probably one of the first church services they have ever been to.

The regulars hug each other and find seats on the green carpet or the various couches. It's time for Mr. Ed! A forty-five-year-old man in a black leather jacket and a bandanna walks out from behind the stage and welcomes everyone. He draws some names from among the newcomer cards, giving away some CDs and a T-shirt.

Mr. Ed launches into his stand-up comedy routine, then several staff interns jump up on stage to perform a comedy skit. Someone announces upcoming concerts and a few birthdays, then the kids bow their heads and prepare themselves for worship. A worship band of talented young people leads several songs as kids throughout the room raise their hands.

After worship, a short video clip introduces the topic for the night. Then the kids hear a message focusing on God's unconditional love for everyone in the room. The interns perform another skit, this time more serious in tone. As the meeting ends, kids have an opportunity to respond to God. Some hearts are touched, tears flow, and the leaders and the interns pray with several teenagers. God has shown up once again to comfort and change these kids. They hug each other as the worship band plays a closing song.

In a short time, the lights will go on again, the coffee bar will reopen, and the young people will hang out, play pool, and talk with their friends. But no one is the same after spending time with the King of Kings.

Who We Are and How It Works

First of all, let me make it clear that Souled Out Ministries is not a separatist ministry in competition with other local churches. We are in place to build a bridge between unchurched teenagers and local churches. We work alongside and with other churches to reach out to young people and to give them ministry opportunities.

After outgrowing our family room years ago, the youth church moved several times. As the ministry grew and a team began to develop, we traveled between abandoned retail stores, a church basement, a school gymnasium, and a mall. After three years, we finally found our own building, which we now own. This building houses all the ministries of Souled Out.

Our doors are open for "Coffee Talk," a student-led Bible study on Tuesday evenings. Our seeker-friendly service, "Souled Out," is on

Thursday nights. Friday nights from 7 p.m. until 1 a.m., we host a coffeehouse for kids. On Saturday afternoons, we have "Get Out," when we work with other ministries to feed the homeless and help the poor in Chicago. On Saturday nights we hold Christian concerts. This is the only night we charge an admission fee. On Sunday nights we have a service called "Get Real," which is basically a church service, featuring worship, teaching, and prayer.

We equip interns and student leaders to work with almost every aspect of the ministry, from maintaining the building to preparing messages. The student leaders are high school students who represent Christ on campus. The interns are college-age young people learning how to work in youth ministry. They teach Bible studies, disciple kids, participate in music and drama, help with special projects, and meet weekly to discuss direction and planning. Alongside this ministry team, we have a student on staff who is about to graduate from college with a degree in youth ministry. He leads our worship team and helps direct our international missions involvement.

Our adult staff includes two pastors. One works with administration and family counseling. The other pastor works as a youth pastor and coordinates all the concerts. My husband and I are the co-directors and founders. We work with the overall planning. Although the adult staff teaches in many of the meetings, we see our primary role as coaches and mentors. Our goal is to help empower this generation, providing opportunities for them to test their wings in a safe environment.

Why a Youth Church?

We chose to form a youth church rather than a parachurch ministry (although we have a strong element of parachurch within our ministry) because Scripture indicates that the church is God's blueprint for the body of Christ. Although parachurch ministries can be very effective, especially when they work together with local youth groups, they're often missing the "family" or "body" element of the local church. Today's young people are looking more than ever for a sense of "family," since families are deteriorating. In a society where so many young people aren't attending church and have little or no knowledge of Scripture, we have tried to find a way to introduce this generation to the concept of the local church within their own culture.

We've focused on developing a youth program that will strengthen other churches in their ministry to teenagers. We have a neutral location, a place where other youth groups can take advantage of any of our activities, where Christians kids can meet together and find strength, and where unchurched young people will come to meet Jesus. Because we want to work with other youth groups, our primary meetings are on Thursday nights and Sunday nights so that they don't conflict with anyone else's meetings. We definitely don't see ourselves as separate or in competition with other churches; we want to work with them to reach out to teenagers.

Kevin

Kevin was an only child. His mother, who had never married, had raised him with very little support. During his younger years she became a Christian and wanted to raise him in a Christian home. She took him to various churches and Sunday schools, but he wouldn't behave. He tested everyone. Several churches encouraged Kevin and his mother to leave because of his misbehavior.

When Kevin hit his teen years, he was sent to a military school, where he lasted one semester. Kevin seemed to have a death wish. He continued to test the limits of everything, now with more and more recklessness. When he first arrived at Souled Out, he didn't necessarily stand out. He often came high, and sometimes after the services he would pick fights. It took several months before we saw a hunger for God in him.

We challenged Kevin with an opportunity to go on our annual mission trip. It was a risk, but the other kids rallied around Kevin, determined to be his friend and to help him accomplish this. We laid out the expectations (getting off drugs, consistently walking with Christ, and giving up smoking for the trip). Kevin came through and went with us! On the trip his fearlessness really was an asset to the rest of the group. He was bold enough to take risks, talking with people no one else would. And he became one of our best street performers.

But when he came home from that trip, Kevin fell back into his old ways. Drugs became his lord once again, and we began to wonder what would happen to Kevin. After several months of coming drunk and high, he finally realized we still loved him and wouldn't desert him. He also realized that if he didn't change, he would die. He got treatment for his drug addiction.

Now Kevin has been clean for over a year. He's in a discipleship program, and his life is taking shape. Today he helps our younger kids who come into Souled Out in the same condition he was in years ago. Kevin is a testimony to the strength of God's unconditional love as well as to the power of knowing that people believed in him.

Unconditional Love and Acceptance

So how do these deeply hurting young people fit into the church? These young people are still in the process of growing and changing. The church can be an example of God's unconditional love and acceptance—a place where they feel accepted no matter how they look or what they've done.

Just because we love and accept kids unconditionally doesn't mean we just let them get away with anything. We confront them constantly. Kevin heard me confront him time and time again. Yet he knew he was accepted, so he kept coming back. Kids come to us high every week. If we kick them out because we don't want them to "influence" the others, they may never learn that God has open arms for them if they really want him. Just a few days ago, a sixteen-year-old cried in our office, ashamed that he had come to Souled Out on drugs. He had been in our prayers for many weeks. When he came in weeping because he was ashamed, we were able to pray with him and lead him back to the Lord.

Drop the Religion and Keep It Simple

If you're trying to build a bridge between unchurched young people and young people from the church, you have to drop the "Christianese." Several years ago, while we were still meeting in our home, my husband opened the Bible and began teaching. We saw blank stares throughout the room as the kids struggled to understand what he was sharing. Many of them had never heard Bible stories and didn't understand biblical principles.

After that meeting, Ed and I prayed to find a way to teach the kids. We were reminded of Mark 12:28-31. When a man asked Jesus what was the most important commandment, Jesus answered, " 'Love the Lord your God with all your heart and with all your soul and with all your mind and with all your strength.' The second is this: 'Love your neighbor as yourself.' "

We began to use this passage as our theme Scripture. When we taught, we kept the messages short and simple, yet hard-hitting. We took a hard look at anything that seemed culturally "religious," dropping doctrinal teaching for the time being and trying hard to present these young people with simple truth.

Over and over, we taught the kids about a personal love relationship with Jesus and worked on finding ways for them to apply their faith. We wanted to teach kids to love their neighbors as themselves, so we partnered with several organizations in Chicago, feeding the homeless and helping the poor.

We found ourselves less concerned whether young people were smoking cigarettes outside and more concerned with how they were doing on the inside. Yet we believe in teaching them an uncompromising message of Jesus as Lord.

Loving God With Your Whole Heart

We base our rules on Mark 12:28-31: "Are you loving the Lord with your whole heart?" we say. We encourage kids to "fall in love" with the King of Kings, knowing that "falling in love" involves respecting and not hurting the one they love. This has opened doors for kids who have no church background to grasp one of the key truths of being a Christian.

One sign that our approach was effective came as a surprise when some kids decided to leave Souled Out. After they quit coming, we asked them what was wrong. They told us they didn't want to follow God. When we asked them why, they replied: "The cost of loving God with my whole heart is too great." Although they knew they were accepted, they also knew about the expectations on their hearts.

Love Your Neighbor as Yourself

Because our churched kids have a foundation, at first they didn't really know how to relate to their peers. They knew the attitudes, language, and behavior of some of the kids were inappropriate. Many weren't sure whether to talk to the other kids or ignore them. Some of our kids were even tempted by some of the baggage other kids came with.

To break down the walls between these two groups of kids, we held retreats, mission trips, and inner city outreaches. But the most effective way to bridge the two groups was to realize they were two groups. We encourage the kids who have strong relationships with God to love and pray for the others. Our ministry team and adults work separately with each of the groups, giving them their own places. We've brought our "core church kids" into roles of leadership and trained them to look at their fellow teenagers as people Jesus loves. We've taught them that Jesus associated with all kinds of people and never compromised. And because our activities and times don't conflict with other church youth groups, those core kids are able to grow spiritually and be discipled in other churches as well as Souled Out.

In reality this takes a lot of adult leadership and communication. Because the young people are looking to the adults for direction, it's very important that adults communicate with the core church kids, reminding them that they're on a mission and helping them develop compassionate hearts for their own generation. The two groups have developed a sense of family—with respect and love for each other because of shared experiences.

Several of the people on our ministry team are assigned to be in the parking lot during services to talk to those who don't come in for meetings. One night as I talked with a group of young people sitting in the parking lot, a boy said to me, "Do you know why it's hard for us to come in?" I asked why, and he said, "Because sometimes we're high, we don't live that good, and we just don't feel worthy."

Later I walked back into the meeting, which happened to be about God's unconditional love and acceptance. At the end of the message, I went up to the front, crying. I told the kids that a group of kids in the parking lot didn't feel worthy to come in. Some of them started to cry, and a large group of teenagers ran outside and talked with them after the service. Soon many of the kids from outside walked into the building and started to play pool and talk.

Now, a few months later, many of these "parking lot kids" have given their hearts to Jesus as a result of feeling loved and accepted by the others. It was this simple truth that helped them open up their hearts to God's unconditional love and acceptance: Love God completely, and love your neighbor as yourself.

The Role of Adults in a Youth Church

In a youth church, kids need adults to provide support and nurture. Finding adults willing to do this has been more of a problem than we ever would've thought. Many adults have been willing to be involved if they could teach or have a hand of authority within the ministry, as if they want to find a ministry for themselves rather than help train young people to find their place in the body of Christ. To be an effective adult in a youth church, the adult must be a coach, not the main player. Adults act as counselors, friends, and guides, or even as loving moms and dads.

We've learned that adults who haven't earned the right to speak into kids' lives are tuned out. Earning the right to speak into their lives means building relationships. When adults earn that right, they have an audience, even if they're poor speakers. Young people are looking for adults who are real, not perfect. They hear lectures all day long in school, and they don't want to hear any more at youth meetings.

We've also found that this young generation is hungry for attention from adults and wants them as friends in their lives. Again and again we've seen how much these kids want to find role models to pattern their lives after. What an awesome responsibility we as adults have in the lives of these young people!

Any adult involved in young people's lives must learn to accept and enjoy teenagers as people. In a society where many young people don't live with their natural fathers or mothers and may never even know them, the church must get into these young lives and become spiritual moms and dads to help restore these kids. We must open our hearts and homes to a generation that is looking for someone to love them. These are the adults we look for—adults without agendas who care about young people and are willing to learn from them.

Do I Have to Open My Home?

Our youth ministry began naturally out of our open-home policy. When our own children began high school, they brought their friends over, and it wasn't long before our home became a place to hang out. We opened our doors, our refrigerator, and our lives to them. It wasn't unusual for lots of kids to come over during their open campus at lunch. We had lots of "strays" at dinner and many kids for the night. I stayed up late with all of them, spending lots of time getting to know them.

The many late nights were a challenge, but I could see that God was doing something because he was bringing kids over all the time. One night we had an overnight with the boys gymnastics team. My daughter had some of her friends staying over too. The girls and the boys launched into silly stories about jobs they had had. I sat on the couch with them, and we laughed. There was such a spirit of joy and innocence, I could tell God was up to something. We laughed so hard, our bellies ached. It was amazing—all these teenagers sitting around with a mom late at night, not swearing or telling coarse jokes, but laughing. Most of these kids weren't Christians, and several of them were pretty tough kids. But that night they found a piece of their innocence. The next day at a gymnastics meet, they all thanked me for the "greatest night they had had in a long time." The following week they came to our youth group, and several of them committed their lives to Jesus. Now several years later, from time to time, some of them still remind me of that night!

It isn't necessary that you open your home for this model to work, but I'm convinced that the most effective way to reach today's young people is by opening your home. I know this can be difficult while raising children (we have four) and trying to spend time with your spouse. But if you can draw boundary lines for yourselves (spending enough time with your spouse and family, keeping family times exclusive, dealing with family concerns in private) and still open your home, you'll find a lot of success in reaching these kids. Keep in mind that when I say, "Open your home," that doesn't mean letting kids walk in and do what they want. Just make them feel like part of your family. Inviting this generation into your lives, being "real" and open with them, is a great way to show young people the love of Christ.

Kids Ministering to Kids

If negative peer pressure can change even the most well-adjusted young person, what can be the effect of positive peer pressure? At a retreat at our home three years ago, we watched the effects of positive peer pressure. We had more than forty-five teenagers sleeping all over our house for the weekend. We had thirteen young people we knew from an Ohio youth group come in to speak for the retreat. They shared from their hearts about the love they had for Jesus. Because they were teenagers, our own group respected and listened to them. They were able to say things we never would have been able to say. They challenged each other as peers. They prayed together and got serious.

That weekend was nothing short of miraculous. Although we all had little sleep, we watched God begin to work in the lives of kids we never thought could be so dramatically touched. On Friday evening a teenage boy stopped at our house, thinking we were having a party. Some of the kids knew him from school and asked him to stay for the meetings. There he heard the gospel for the first time, shared by someone his own age. He cried, not even knowing why, and ended up staying the entire weekend. He committed his life to Jesus and opened his first Bible. He cried when he read it, and the others surrounded him with hugs. Today he is still following God and works with our worship team.

We saw in action the awesome power of kids ministering to kids. Ever since that time, when we want to discuss difficult topics, we call on other young people to help speak. As they speak with their own generation, they are able to say much more than we as leaders feel free to say.

Our Own Personal Treasures

Don't overlook the fact that there is a treasure in your young people. Each one has something significant to say. Youth leaders who don't equip young people to do ministry are missing the joy of seeing what's inside of them, not to mention cutting off some of the effectiveness they can bring to a group.

One week a musician who was scheduled to speak and perform at our Souled Out service missed his airline connection. He called us and told us he would be at the meeting an hour late. That particular week, an entire seminary class was coming to check us out, wanting to know what we were all about. Well, with half an hour's notice, we had to come up with a complete change of plans for the music and the message. So we asked three of our young people to share what Jesus had meant in their lives. One was a new Christian who had been a heroin addict. Another had known Jesus most of his life. The third was a young girl who had left her home at the age of sixteen.

No one was ready for the power of the stories from these three young people. At the end there wasn't a dry eye in the place. The seminary students were amazed at the wealth within our kids. God had used the treasure we had in our own ministry.

Challenges of a Youth Church

Probably one of the greatest challenges of a youth church is the fact that the teenagers grow up and move on to college. Kids don't stay kids for long. After they graduate from high school, they're gone, usually to college. And we have the problem of finding a place for them to fit when they come back. If we target high school kids, college kids will eventually be left out. But if we target college kids, we'll lose the high school students.

In our Thursday night meetings, we'll always maintain a strong high school emphasis. But in our Sunday night service, we've been working to develop a program that accommodates more of the needs of college-age students and older young people who come to Souled Out.

When a young person from an unchurched background becomes a Christian, they have no church home to go to. On some occasions we refer kids to other churches, but basically we are their church. We hope that because we've introduced them to a church family, these young people will be able to integrate into other churches as they become adults. We're still figuring out how to help kids from Souled Out plug into other churches, but that's our goal.

Another challenge we've encountered has come from the Christian community. Recently a Christian college professor made a negative statement in his class regarding our ministry. Some of the students called us, quite alarmed. I had never met the man, and as far as I know, he had never come to check out what we were doing. We become frustrated when other Christians fail to come to us with their concerns. Many people assume that because we're a youth church, we're in opposition to other churches and youth ministry programs. On the contrary, we work together with many churches to do ministry, and we try to schedule our events so that they don't conflict with events at other churches. We're doing ministry the best way we can to reach a segment of young people many churches are missing, but we've felt very much alone while fighting for this generation. The body of Christ would be so much more effective if we could all work together.

To try to build bridges, we contact other youth groups to let them know who we are and what we have available. We're thrilled when other youth groups join us for activities and use our facilities. We also publicize our events and try to partner with other ministries to show God's love to teenagers.

How to Start Your Own Youth Church

If I were to boil it down to a formula, here are the steps I'd say you would need to take to develop a youth church.

Determine the need.

Obviously, the first thing is to look around your community and determine the need for something as unique as a youth church. If you see that the young people need a place to call their own, this might be the route to take. Get all the information and statistics you can. Ask kids lots of questions. This will help you get a glimpse of what God sees when he looks at your community.

Pray like crazy.

Take a look at the statistics concerning young people in your community; they'll bring you to your knees quickly. Nothing great in the kingdom of God happens without first being bathed in prayer. All your greatest efforts will mean absolutely nothing without God breathing life into what you're doing. We have seen God answer us again and again because of his longing for these kids to know him. He wants the job done more than we do!

Find people of like mind, and give your kids ownership.

Obviously you need a team of adults with the same vision you have. But remember, you also need young people with like minds. And you want young people who want ownership of that vision. Bring them in on your prayer and planning times. Make them a team, and be their coach. God is into teamwork!

You may want to look to a team of several churches to join you in launching this ministry. Establishing partnerships now will increase your effectiveness later.

Find a neutral setting kids will want to be in.

Remember that in order to bring in young people who have never heard the gospel, you must find a neutral setting. Many unchurched young people won't hang out in a church basement. When we met in a church basement for six months while we were between locations, we lost 50 percent of our kids. Although some of them who had never walked on church property continued to show up, most of them didn't. Although we want to partner with other churches in ministry, we are a separate church, and many of our kids won't go to traditional church buildings.

And don't forget to make your meeting place a place kids want to be! The building you meet in will reflect the kind of attitude you have toward young people. We decided to make our building very contemporary and homey instead of giving kids a warehouse and letting them live with old couches and broken chairs. Instead, the colors are coordinated and the furniture is new. Several of the young people and interns helped paint and decorate. When we first opened our building, a group of rough young people who had been starting to come to Souled Out walked in and said, "This is for us?" One of them even began to cry! They couldn't believe people cared enough about them to give them a place that nice. Why should we leave the leftovers to our young people? Show them how valuable they are!

Raise money, and sacrifice.

People often ask us, "Who funds this thing?" Obviously with staff and a building, we have many expenses. We've been working to make this ministry self-sufficient. We do hold concerts once a week where we charge admission fees, and currently those fees are covering the cost of the concerts with some left over. We also have a coffee bar whose proceeds help with our utility bills. We get some donations from local churches. We teach the kids to tithe, and that provides money in the offering each week. We sell T-shirts and jewelry and have a small bookstore.

But the way God has met most of our financial needs is through donations from the business community. We spend a lot of time talking with area business people and sharing with them our dream. It didn't take long to find like-minded individuals with a heart for young people.

Recently, a youth leader from Michigan came to visit us, asking us how to run a youth church. We asked him where he was meeting, and he told us a local businessman had just given him a warehouse! Don't be afraid to talk to everyone about your idea—you just don't know what might be out there if you ask.

When we looked for our building, we had a problem with zoning. There were plenty of buildings available, but none were zoned for a "youth church." Because of our zoning problems, a local newspaper ran a story calling us a "nomadic youth ministry." We called village officials, asking them for help. We finally found an official in a neighboring community who had a heart for young people. He had read the story, and he helped us meet all the zoning requirements so we were able to find a building.

The building we found was perfect, but the price was way beyond our budget. We approached the owner for half the price with a tax-deductible receipt. God moved in the heart of the owner, and he accepted our offer. But then we had to come up with the down payment! We prayed, and days later we received a phone call from a local businessman who had heard about our group and gave us the down payment as his donation. Don't underestimate the love God has for this generation!

Work with a team to develop strong programs.

Make sure you include your teenagers in your planning! They'll help you understand what really works to bring kids closer to God. We try to give them so many experiences with God, we spoil them for the ordinary. Now kids who have come through Souled Out have had so many good meetings, missions opportunities, relationships, and concerts that they won't settle for ho-hum Christianity. The experience of growing in their faith drives these young people to become leaders in other churches as they make the transition into adulthood.

Contact neighboring youth groups.

We try very hard not to compete with other ministries but instead complement what they're doing to reach young people. We love having a place other youth groups can use. On coffeehouse nights and on concert nights, lots of different youth groups come in.

The body of Christ is much stronger when we're in unity, not fighting each other. Reach out to your neighboring youth ministries, and keep them informed of any special events you might be planning. The kids don't care what church other kids go to; they just want to meet other Christian kids. They want to not be alone in their faith.

Contact high schools and junior high schools.

What a helping hand we can be to our communities if we partner with them instead of deserting them. This may take a lot of divine intervention, but in the long run, working with schools in the area will open doors to many kids' lives! Currently we're opening our stage to various high schools so their choir groups can use our sound system. We feel that anything that acts as a bridge between us and the community is of great value. Be creative in inviting schools to experience your ministry. If you keep that door open to them, they'll keep their doors open to you.

Invite the kids!

If you have a youth group with its own place and its own programs, and you see kids standing on the street corners with nothing to do, *ask them in!* Don't be intimidated by their lifestyle. They need you. Open your doors to the kids in the malls and the convenience stores. Teach your student leaders to bring in everyone they know.

Create an environment God can work in.

Don't be afraid to share the gospel with this young generation. Don't tiptoe around, giving them a soft gospel message. Teach them that Jesus is Lord, and give them a challenge. Make sure you present plenty of opportunities for the kids to make things right with God. Although you want to accept everyone, you also want to give them alternatives to the lifestyles they're trapped in. If you aren't convinced that Jesus is the answer for them, they won't be. Show them that you're in love with Jesus, in love with prayer, and in love with God's ways. This is the environment God uses to change the lives of people.

In Conclusion

It's late on a Tuesday afternoon, and the adult leaders and interns from the ministry team are starting their weekly planning meeting. The phone keeps ringing. There isn't a lot of time—soon other ministry team leaders will be coming in to prepare for the Bible study that will begin in a few hours. My husband, Ed, who is actually a businessman and runs Souled Out in his "spare time," has just arrived.

"Hey, gang," he says, "How's it going? OK, let's get started!" He opens his overflowing briefcase and pulls out copies of the latest thought-provoking article on young people. We begin in prayer. We discuss the topic for Thursday night. We go over last-minute plans.

Scott, our youth pastor and concert coordinator, has a question about some video clips. Jen and August, our college interns who are more like our daughters, discuss a skit together. Josh, our student on staff, talks about the worship plans. JJ, a high school student leader, gives the teenage point of view. Joe, the pastor, who has been working with us for over a year, discusses how we can get more involved in the high schools. "Have we spent too much time on the concerts?" he asks. The debate is on the table, and we all offer our opinions.

For a moment, as the phones are ringing and the creative energy is flowing, I stop and remember that one Wednesday night a few years ago. How vividly I can recall the way I felt when our pastor and his assistant left our home that night. I was heartbroken, and I knew things would never be the same. But as I look across the conference table on this Tuesday night, I smile, grateful to the God who loves this generation. And I thank God that Joe—our former pastor—is now sitting on staff with us.

CHAPTER 7:
On-Campus Missionaries

Campus-Based Youth Ministry

MONTY L. HIPP
National Director for Youth Alive in Springfield, Missouri

with MIKAL KEEFER

I t's early on a Thursday morning, and the student parking lot at Everett High School is just beginning to fill. A small group of teenagers walks slowly around the outside of the school building, quietly asking God to direct everything that happens inside the walls of this public school.

At noon another group of teenagers will meet to "pray through the yearbook," while dozens of other Christians invite non-Christian friends to join them for lunch in the cafeteria.

All this is happening at a school that has no organized Christian club on campus...and no youth worker in sight.

• • • • • • • •

What's Right About Public Schools in America

There's no shortage of complaints about public schools in America. Test scores are slipping. New schools are expensive. Teachers don't seem able to care the way they did back in the good old days. The list goes on, and Christians often add a few more items to the list: Schools don't encourage prayer or Bible study. They teach evolution as fact. Drugs, sex, and rock 'n' roll have overrun middle and high school campuses and turned them into cesspools of sin.

However, the public school remains one of the finest ideas God ever put into the hearts of people. Why? Because every school day, schools are packed with *students*.

Some students in your local schools know God. Others don't. But the students are *there*—sitting in classes, jostling through crowded hallways.

These students are poised to make commitments to follow Jesus. Studies indicate that more than 80 percent of the people who become Christians do so before they turn twenty years old.[1] And there they are—all in one place, at one time, every school day.

The public high school is a tremendous mission field, and for many churches one that's literally across the street or down the block. So why aren't more churches targeting public school campuses for outreach and evangelism?

Youth ministry in the coming decade can't afford to miss this opportunity. And neither can youth ministers who want to see students in their groups grow in faith and servanthood.

But be aware that effective campus ministry today doesn't look like campus ministry in the past few decades. Back then, campus ministry usually meant forming a club. Most of the club's members were churched students who wanted to do something at school. It was a rallying place for Christian students.

Today campus ministry is like being on a mission field—presenting Christ to teenagers who have had little or no personal exposure to the gospel.

The emphasis has shifted from maintaining Christian students in their faith to actively reaching out in evangelism. Evangelism must be a major strategic element of youth ministry programs. Youth workers must disciple teenagers to reach out to their friends at school.

Do it, and the results can be staggering.

Fail to disciple your teenagers and you'll not only miss an opportunity, you'll also shortchange them.

Campus Ministry Makes Sense—for Your Students and Your Church

Your students, both middle schoolers and high school students, can be a powerful force on their campuses *if* they see school as a mission field rather than just a place to show up day after day.

Your students are perfectly positioned to be campus missionaries. They have relationships with non-Christian teenagers. They share lockers with non-Christian students, eat lunch with them, and run around the track with them in gym class. And they understand the pressures every teenager faces daily.

The good news is that your teenagers are already looking for a worthy cause. They want something to live for and to pour their lives into. They want to champion a cause that makes a significant difference.

Ministry to their friends at school is that cause. Christian students can make an eternal difference in the lives of their friends.

When your students begin enthusiastically sharing their faith at school, good things will happen in your church youth group as well as in the schools. Your group will shift into high gear. You'll see students dive into Bible study because they see immediate relevance in knowing God's Word. And you'll build your youth ministry on a sense of mission, not on a personality or a program.

Consider what's happening in Glendale, Arizona, where youth pastor Philip Owens coordinates campus ministry efforts in four area schools.

"My students' involvement in campus ministry has helped them grow tremendously," Owens says. "When students invite friends and see results, they're encouraged. The Christian students see that they are examples in their schools, so they step up their Christian walk. And they study more because they're answering friends' questions. They know they have to be prepared."

The difference in Owens' youth group is nothing less than spectacular. He says, "When you launch a campus ministry, you see faithfulness and commitment increase in every area of your students' lives. They feel more urgency to share their faith. And they learn to worship."

Here's another benefit: Teenagers learn to enter into worship, share their faith with their friends, and embrace discipleship *without* a youth worker present.

The Youth Leader's Role

In a campus-ministry approach to youth ministry, it's the youth leader's job to instill in students a passion for sharing their faith. As a youth leader, you're the catalyst, the initial link between your church and the missionary project. You're also a coach, model, and mentor — communicating a vision for reaching non-Christians and discipling your young people for spiritual growth.

Effective campus ministry isn't a solo project. In fact, you *can't* be the one up front in campus ministry. For starters, it may be illegal for you to set foot on a school campus, let alone to share your faith there. Public Law No. 98-377, commonly known as the Equal Access Act, authorizes religious clubs on public secondary campuses — but only if the meetings are student initiated and voluntary, and only if non-school personnel (that's you, youth worker) don't direct, conduct, control, or regularly attend the meetings and activities.

Although you may never set foot on a school campus to do direct ministry, you'll be active in encouraging and preparing teenagers to do ministry. Effective campus ministry always begins with teenagers who care deeply about sharing their faith.

In short, this is your students' show. Your role is to motivate and provide training. It's essential that you involve your students, and it's equally *essential* that you involve the adults in your church.

Guess Who's Coming to the Potluck?

Campus ministries that make a longterm difference follow a simple pattern: They reach non-Christian teenagers at school, and then they disciple them in the context of local churches.

For an unchurched teenager, a Bible club at school or a parachurch Christian club meeting on Monday night has an impact. Parachurch organizations operating on campuses have literally changed lives.

But once students graduate, they don't always make the move from parachurch ministries to local churches. The vast majority of students in parachurch ministries are temporary recruits to the kingdom.

It's time for parachurch ministries and local churches to forge partnerships that enhance their impact on campuses.

Think of what would happen if local churches provided support and mentoring to young people reached through parachurch ministries. Connecting teenagers to healthy local churches for continued spiritual development must become a priority. But involving unchurched teenagers in local congregations can be more challenging than it might appear.

Most churches say they want teenagers reached for Jesus. You'd think a youth worker who finds a way to double or triple a youth group would get a round of applause or maybe a raise—at least an off-street parking spot.

But having a herd of unchurched teenagers suddenly invade a cozy church can be awkward. These kids know almost nothing about the Bible and even less about church-service etiquette. They may raise their hands to ask questions during sermons. They may head off to the bathroom during the Lord's Supper. And a lifetime of questionable vocabulary doesn't disappear overnight.

If you intend to do campus ministry, you need the support and involvement of your church for a number of reasons—not the least of which is that if you're successful, some interesting students will be showing up for the next church potluck.

Campus ministry is not a small undertaking. Before you announce the grand opening of your new ministry to schools, lay a solid foundation by taking the following six steps.

Step 1: Pray fervently for your schools and the students in them.

Ask God what he wants to do in your local schools. Ask how God intends to reach students with his grace. And make yourself completely available to do what he asks. Lay aside your ego, and be open to the possibility that it may be best to not create your own program but to join an existing work.

Step 2: Get your teenagers on board.

Prepare a nucleus of students who are ready to openly represent Christ on their school campuses. For a campus ministry to have impact, your students *must*

- believe that their non-Christian friends need Jesus Christ and
- feel a personal spiritual responsibility to share their faith with their friends.

Evangelism runs counter to popular culture. In a world that's increasingly inclusive and politically correct, many teenagers are hesitant to take Jesus at his word that he is the only way to God (John 11:25-27). But until they believe what Jesus said, they probably will have little motivation to share the Christian faith with friends.

Your teenagers must also move from good intentions to a purposeful action plan for evangelism. Unless they fervently embrace the need for evangelism, your students' missionary efforts on campus will fail. It's that simple.

Where there's effective campus ministry two elements are *always* present: prayer for people who don't know Jesus, and students who view themselves as missionaries on their school campuses.

Step 3: Convince your church that school campuses are mission fields.

Invite your senior pastor and key members of your church leadership to join you at "See You at the Pole" or another on-campus outreach event. Buy them breakfast and provide transportation if necessary. Do everything short of an outright kidnapping to get these leaders on campus to see teenagers sharing their faith.

Don't skip this step! The greatest single thing that can happen for your campus ministry is for local church leaders to see public school campuses as part of the church's overall missions strategy.

When schools are classified as mission fields, doors open and resources appear. The responsibility for campus ministry is shared and no longer solely on your shoulders. And you're in position to ask for funding.

That's right: You need to ask for money, and from the *missions budget,* no less. But before you do, be sure as many influential people as possible share your vision for campus ministry. These people will sell the idea for you.

By the way, while you're at it, find out what it would take to get a teenager on the missions committee.

Step 4: Ask for money—from the missions budget.

No matter how well-funded your youth ministry is, *ask for money from your church's missions budget.*

Why? Because with the money come some other very important things: respect, visibility, and volunteer support. As an official church missions project, your campus ministry—along with the students who serve as campus missionaries—will be taken seriously.

Remember that many adults in your church are or have been the parents of teenagers or expect to be. Once they see results, they'll champion your cause.

And the results can be impressive. Your teenagers' faith will deepen. They'll actively participate in the life of the church. And any adults who are suspicious of teenagers will discover renewed faith in the next generation.

For an effective campus ministry, you *must* have the involvement of your church. You need Christian adults gifted in evangelism to share their expertise. You need Sunday school teachers to help train your teenagers. And you need adult mentors to step forward.

Besides, reaching out to non-Christian teenagers is a legitimate mission. And in this type of outreach, church members can see, touch, and directly impact people who need to know Jesus.

Step 5: Bring your community together around campus ministry.

Let's admit it: We all love running successful programs—especially programs that get admired. And we're often distrustful of other churches and ministries who tread on our turf.

It's time to set aside ego when it comes to campus ministries.

For campus ministries to work in the twenty-first century, it's critical that local churches and parachurch organizations work together. The current generation of teenagers doesn't have denominational affiliation. Students move across party lines without a second thought. Teenagers connect to causes, not denominations, so it makes absolutely no sense to have sixteen separate ministries on campus—each with three students.

It's better for every organization with an interest in campus ministry to focus on common core values shared by evangelical churches. The payoff comes when a teenager who attends a parachurch ministry meeting and a prayer breakfast sponsored by a local church hears the same truth presented in both places: Jesus came, died in our place, and wants us to accept his free gift of eternal life.

The public school campus is a common denominator for every ministry in your community. You all want to reach teenagers, and your common bond is that you all want students to commit themselves to personal relationships with Jesus Christ.

For the sake of the teenagers we want to reach, our diversity cannot continue to divide us.

Step 6: Make campus ministry part of your ministry philosophy.

You're asking your teenagers for a lot of commitment when they become campus missionaries. You owe it to them to believe so deeply in this approach to evangelism that it becomes part of your life.

That means deciding you love teenagers enough to disciple them, train them, and debrief what they experience as campus missionaries. You must show that you love them enough to provide the support they need to serve on the front lines of ministry.

Be willing to take this one to the mat. Campus ministry isn't a halfway program. You must be *passionate* about your students sharing their faith.

Counting the Cost

Tom Bachman, statewide director of Youth Alive in Oregon, suggests each teenager make the following five commitments before being commissioned as a campus missionary:

● commit to pray for his or her school and the students and staff in it,

● agree to live a lifestyle that reflects Christ's love for others,

● join with other Christians in a campus club or seek to start one,

● select five friends for a personal evangelism focus, and

● faithfully participate in supporting his or her home church's missions.

This kind of commitment doesn't happen by accident. It requires constant prayer support and deliberate nurturing as well as adult supervision.

There's no question about whether campus ministries work—they do! The process of discipling students to share their faith with others is based on an approach that was used by Jesus himself.

And there's no question about what happens to teenagers who decide to obey and follow Jesus. It brings them into relationship with Christ, and their spiritual growth increases dramatically.

Consider campus ministry for your church. The schools need you. The students need you.

Tips From the Trenches

Here are some tips from people who are involved in a campus-ministry approach to youth ministry. Plug these into your campus ministry planning.

Divide and conquer.

Tom Bachman recommends implementing a four-pronged strategy for campus ministry.

● PRAYER GROUPS—Set up these groups to meet before, during, or after school.

● ACCOUNTABILITY GROUPS—Students in these groups hold each other accountable regarding prayer and Bible reading. These groups should be open to non-Christians. They start with three students; then each student tries to recruit one to three other students to join the group for lunch in the cafeteria.

● AN ON-CAMPUS CLUB—A club gives focus to missionary efforts and provides a nonthreatening place for new Christians. Encourage your kids to either join an existing club or start their own.

● TARGET GROUPS—Identify campus groups for missionary efforts. Host a pizza lunch for freshmen or for everyone in the music department. Ask parents to host a potluck for teachers and adult staff, and ask Christian staff members or students to briefly tell what God has done in their lives. Make it a goal to clearly present the gospel at least twice to everyone on campus.

The benefit of using more than one approach is that if one strategy fails, the others keep the ministry growing. No club allowed on campus? Not a problem—prayer and accountability groups will keep campus missionaries motivated and working. Missing a prayer group? The club will keep things moving along.

Be true to your school.

Look for times during the school year when your church can support schools and their student bodies. For instance, when schools have fund-raisers, make donations from your missions budget to the projects of your choice.

Why is this important? Because when school administrations recognize that your church supports their educational goals and mission, the school administration will be responsive when you seek to provide positive input into the lives of students.

Schools are constantly in need of support, and they want to know the community is behind them. When you help your community's schools in practical ways, you'll discover that the schools speak highly of your church and ministry. Be aware, though, that it's particularly important to provide support long *before* you ask for anything!

Dedicate your campus missionaries.

Treat teenagers who accept a calling to campus ministry the way you'd treat any other missionary. Commission them publicly on a Sunday morning. Encourage them. Place their pictures on the missionary bulletin board beside the picture of the couple serving in Taiwan. And ask campus missionaries to send regular reports to the missions committee, outlining plans and results.

Request prayer in your church bulletin. Ask campus missionaries which school friends they're praying for—and put those names on your church's prayer list. You'll see powerful things happen, and you'll build awareness that campus ministry is about reaching students with the gospel.

Use on-campus meetings...but don't rely on them.

Currently, the law protects your students' right to meet at school. But laws change, and students' ability to form Christian student clubs may disappear at any time. If your campus ministry depends on on-campus meetings, the ministry will end the day meetings are canceled.

But if you've discipled students to be personally committed to sharing their faith one-on-one, ministry will continue. Build up your teenagers to be missionaries, and your campus ministry won't depend on the whim of the school district or the legislature.

On-site clubs can be part of your campus missions strategy, but not *all* of it. Instead, concentrate on presenting Christ's love on campus, and use every avenue available to you...especially sending teenage missionaries onto campus.

Train your students continually.

Be sure your students have the Bible knowledge and prayer support they need. Make sure they aren't eaten alive on campus. Periodic and ongoing training seminars work better than trying to cram everything in their heads before releasing them to ministry.

Remember, teenagers are in a time of perpetual change and turmoil. They need constant reinforcement and support. You can't give them a one-night campaign speech and then send them off to be on their own for six months. Training isn't a one-shot deal.

Don't neglect middle schools to focus completely on high schools.

Middle schoolers and junior highers are excellent at accepting missionary roles because they're searching for identity. They like identifying with a particular cause and mission. And they not only believe the gospel, they also believe in serving others.

It's dangerous to ignore the younger age group. They're ready, and the need on middle school campuses is real. And if middle school young people see themselves as campus missionaries, they'll have the chance to serve for at least five years on a mission field before graduating from high school.

When presenting campus ministry to your church, find a spokesperson.

Sure, you're a great person and a powerful communicator, but you're always asking for volunteers, right? So give it a rest here, and get someone else to rally the troops. Recruit an influential businessperson from the church, a parent, or a church leader to say, "I want to tell you why this is important."

One live zealot can accomplish more than any ten comatose committees.

Consider campus ministry a litmus test.

You may go through all these steps and discover you're unable to change the philosophy of your church leadership. If your passion to reach teenagers on campus is too great to let go, move on—before you become frustrated beyond repair.

Making a Difference

Campus-based youth ministry is changing lives. Jonathan Holiman, a youth pastor in Sandy, Oregon, describes the difference in his community as "an explosion in evangelism." His church started out with three student missionaries at the beginning of the school year, and now they're down to one. But the other students are getting excited about on-campus ministry. The students are sharing their faith, and many of their peers are committing themselves to Jesus. Holiman hopes to commission fifteen to twenty new missionaries during an upcoming Sunday service.

Jenny Smith is a campus missionary at Sandy High School. Her best friend—one of the friends she focused her outreach efforts on—was baptized in the morning service at her church last Sunday. Jenny is thrilled at seeing God's hand work through her ministry: "I am so thankful for God's touch. I continue to pray for his blessings, and I give praise to his name each and every day. Thank you, Jesus!"

Maybe campus-based youth ministry can make this kind of change in the students in your church and community.

ENDNOTES

1. Thom S. Rainer, The Bridger Generation (Nashville, TN: Broadman & Holman, 1997), 166.